FEDERICO GARCIA LORCA

Poésies II

Chansons
Poème du Cante Jondo
Romancero gitan

TRADUIT DE L'ESPAGNOL
PAR A. BELAMICH, P. DARMANGEAT
J. SUPERVIELLE ET J. PRÉVOST
PRÉFACE
DE JEAN CASSOU

GALLIMARD

PRÉFACE

*Le printemps de 1931 qui vit la chute d'Alphonse XIII
et l'avènement de la République espagnole s'accompagna,
dans les années qui avaient précédé le 14 avril et celles qui
le suivirent, d'une autre belle saison, un long printemps
poétique. Tout un groupe de jeunes poètes, Federico Garcia
Lorca, Pedro Salinas, Jorge Guillén, Rafael Alberti,
José Bergamin, Luis Cernuda, Manuel Altolaguirre,
Damaso Alonso, Vicente Aleixandre, tant d'autres encore,
avait succédé aux maîtres de la fameuse génération de 98,
elle-même riche en grands lyriques, Unamuno, Machado,
et au maître altier, solitaire et pur de la génération inter-
médiaire, Juan Ramon Jiménez. Le coup d'État de Franco
interrompit cette brillante renaissance des lettres espa-
gnoles. La plupart de ces écrivains sont morts en exil ou y
poursuivent leur œuvre. Miguel de Unamuno est mort en
zone franquiste, à Salamanque, gardé à vue dans sa maison
après avoir été frappé en plein visage de ce cri d'un général
rebelle : « Mort à l'intelligence ! ». Antonio Machado a
suivi dans sa déroute l'armée républicaine jusqu'à Col-
lioure où il s'est abattu, où il est enterré, en exil lui aussi.
C'est en exil, un peu avant de s'éteindre, que Juan Ramon
Jiménez a reçu le prix Nobel. Federico Garcia Lorca a*

été fusillé par les troupes franquistes, lors de leur entrée à Grenade, sa patrie, tout au début de la guerre civile.

Il faut rappeler ces événements pour situer la révolution spirituelle de l'Espagne de la fin du XIXe siècle et du commencement du XXe, en donner à sentir l'élan vital, la puissance créatrice, en déplorer la soudaine et irrémédiable cassure. C'est une histoire inachevée, demeurée en suspens et sur la clarté de laquelle la brutale et sanglante réalité projette une ombre sarcastique. Une telle considération se fait plus douloureuse encore quand on la fixe particulièrement sur ce que fut le mouvement poétique de Federico Garcia Lorca et de ses amis. Car on ne saurait imaginer brigade de poètes plus fraternelle, ni emportée par une plus généreuse impatience inventive. De tous ces inspirés Federico était le plus inspiré, le plus aimant aussi et le plus aimé, le plus rayonnant. Celui d'entre tous chez qui, peut-être, se manifestait de la manière la plus vive, la plus efficace cette conviction exaltante que faire œuvre de poésie, c'est faire œuvre d'amitié, d'amitié avec les proches et avec tous, œuvre de relation humaine, de communion populaire, et que c'était bien à cette dernière génération, parvenue au bord du suprême espoir, qu'il appartenait de poursuivre la tâche des glorieux aînés : retrouver l'âme de l'Espagne, renouer avec le génie de l'Espagne, son génie authentique, oublié, en remettre les valeurs en lumière. C'est dans cet esprit que Federico avait créé son théâtre ambulant de la Barraca, participant ainsi à l'entreprise de tant d'étudiants et d'enseignants de l'ère républicaine en vue de ranimer, dans les villages, la musique immémoriale des diverses Espagnes, d'y représenter les pièces du vieux répertoire, Lope, Tirso, Calderon, d'y répandre les belles images du Greco et de Goya. Cette enthousiaste croisade faisait suite à la grande réforme pédagogique, scolaire, universitaire, courageusement commencée, un demi-siècle plus tôt, par d'admirables maîtres qui avaient rêvé une Espagne moderne, réintégrée à la civilisation universelle.

Federico Garcia Lorca était andalou. Qui en eût douté à son premier abord? Cela sautait aux yeux : sa gentillesse d'allure, son alacrité, ce teint de bronze, cette voix de bronze, la drôlerie tout ensemble candide et subtile de ses propos, et puis la tendresse de ses lettres, sa virtuosité en tout, ses dons de musicien, de pianiste, de peintre, de récitant, tout cela était andalou, typiquement andalou, l'Andalousie même. Pas de meilleure occasion, par conséquent, de liquider un exaspérant malentendu : celui du pittoresque andalou, dont on a fait le pittoresque espagnol pour enfin réduire à celui-ci toute l'Espagne. Simplification à jamais fixée et qui satisfait et ravit tout le monde : j'ai dit quelque part que c'était la faute à Carmen. En effet, les chants et les danses des gitans, la guitare, le cante jondo, les castagnettes, un certain tour passionné, sans compter, pour sûr, la semaine sainte à Séville et la feria qui la suit : autant de productions andalouses et qui, comme telles, ont bénéficié d'un énorme succès de vulgarisation. C'est-à-dire qu'elles ont été façonnées en autant de vulgarités. Articles de bazar, attractions de tourisme. Le tourisme, c'est la consommation collective de choses qui ne sauraient être goûtées et appréciées que par la sensibilité individuelle. Ainsi les merveilles de l'Andalousie ne devraient-elles être connues que du voyageur. Mais le voyageur est un type disparu, auquel s'est substitué le touriste ou plutôt les touristes, le troupeau des touristes. Et à cette masse informe et hideuse on offre des exhibitions là où le voyageur cherchait à entendre une confidence. Barrès a bien rencontré lorsqu'il a appliqué le mot de secret à Tolède et au Greco. Si nous

7

ne délivrons pas l'*Andalousie* de la horde tourbillonnante de rengaines et de dégustateurs de rengaines qui la garde captive, si nous ne la lavons pas des vulgarités qui la souillent, si nous ne la considérons pas comme une confidence, comme un secret, nous ne pourrons jamais comprendre Lorca.

Quel est le secret de l'*Andalousie* ? Quelle est cette fonction particulière, spécifique qu'elle exerce ? En quoi consiste son art ? Cet art se résume d'un mot : séduction. C'est un art de séduire. Le coup de reins de la danseuse, le coup de gorge du chanteur, la brusque lueur d'une étoile ou d'un œillet dans une copla funèbre, le manège d'approches et de feintes par quoi le torero conduit sa bête à la mort : autant de charmes qui s'emploient à fasciner les sens et envelopper l'âme, la contraindre, la subjuguer. Et tous ces charmes se résument en un seul, souverain, indéfinissable : la grâce.

Jorge Guillén en vient à nommer la même puissance lorsque, dans la préface à un recueil de sa correspondance avec son ami Federico, il parle de cette « créature extra-ordinaire » en ajoutant : « Créature, cette fois, signifie plus qu'homme. Car Federico nous mettait en contact avec la Création, avec cet ensemble de fond où se maintiennent les forces fécondes, et cet homme était avant tout source, très frais arrachement de source, une transparence d'origine parmi les origines de l'univers... » Cette identification au point des origines, cette résorption d'une manière d'être dans l'être primordial, cette immédiateté font le caractère privilégié de la poésie de Lorca. Elle est pure et simple émanation. C'est pourquoi elle communique une telle impression de joie.

Dans certaines parties de l'œuvre, cette joie de produire s'ébat avec une folle prodigalité, accumule des images saugrenues, les fait rebondir les unes sur les autres : on peut là déceler quelque chose de ce surréalisme qui, en Espagne, mais surtout, en Amérique Latine, s'est traduit, sous les noms d'ultraïsme ou de créationisme, par une étourdissante rhétorique. Mais chez Lorca ces surenchères de libres, extravagantes images témoignent surtout, et une fois de plus, de cette nature de source que Guillén avait définie en lui : il arrive que la source se fasse torrent. Mais elle reste pure, elle reste innocente. Et pour heureuse que soit l'âme du poète, elle n'en est pas moins capable de souffrir de certains heurts, de certains chocs, de certains douloureux accidents et déchirements, de certaines violences et cruautés. Ici nous touchons à un trait capital de la sensibilité de Lorca : sa vulnérabilité. Justement parce qu'innocent, totalement innocent, adorablement ingénu, le poète, plus que tout autre, ressent le tragique du monde.

Essentiellement originel et innocent, Federico se confond avec cette force la plus originelle et innocente qui soit : le peuple. Et dans l'âme du peuple la tragédie du monde produit le même effet que dans l'âme exquise du poète : elle l'atteint au plus vif. Le peuple risque sans cesse son destin et sans cesse tremble pour son destin ; la tragédie est suspendue sur sa tête. Elle va le frapper, et ce sera un abominable désastre.

Donc si Lorca est à ce point originel et innocent, à ce point pur, s'il est au commencement de toutes les choses, s'il est la source d'où, avec un tel naturel, émane une telle abondance de poésie, c'est qu'il est peuple. Mais tout génie espagnol est peuple, tout génie espagnol est le peuple espagnol. Gongora, une de ces gloires radicales de l'Espagne que l'Espagne nouvelle et particulièrement la génération de son compatriote andalou Lorca avait remises à l'honneur, fut sans doute un poète terriblement savant et compliqué : mais aussi l'auteur d'innombrables romances populaires, et, à y bien regarder, son œuvre en style précieux est elle-même populaire et répond à une certaine façon essentielle qu'a le peuple espagnol de penser et de s'exprimer ; si étrange que cela paraisse, le peuple espagnol est naturellement conceptiste. Et le poète espagnol pense et s'exprime populairement, et en cela il est vrai, assuré d'être vrai, strictement vrai, absolument vrai, vrai comme l'eau, comme la terre, comme la mort. Car, ainsi que l'a dit Antonio Machado en une maxime, ou concept, dont le synthétisme péremptoire peut surprendre, mais procède de la plus profonde et juste méditation, « tout ce qui n'est pas folklore est plagiat ». N'oublions pas que Don Quichotte, c'est (entre autres choses, bien sûr, et toutes très importantes, mais celle-là aussi très importante) un recueil de proverbes. Le folkloriste, c'est-à-dire le sociologue, l'ethnologue, celui qui fait du peuple objet de science, parcourt les provinces pour ramasser des proverbes. Le poète, lui, ne se livre point à ces investigations méthodiques : il crée un personnage pour le faire parler en proverbes. Ou bien c'est lui-même qui parle un langage de même sorte. Mais de toutes façons, directement ou par l'intermédiaire de Sancho, c'est lui qui est peuple. Ainsi Federico était-il peuple lorsque, avec son maître Manuel de Falla, il étudiait les très anciens et mystérieux principes du cante jondo et lorsque toute cette musique revivait en lui, dans sa chair et son geste, pour enfin prendre figure dans les rythmes, les images, tous les jaillissements de son prodigieux Romancero gitan.

Une source, en effet, ce miracle d'une source, cette toute première, naïve, sacrée émanation de vie, telle est la poésie de Lorca. Le peuple y coule de source, et le génie. Quel bonheur ! Mais, répétons-le, ce bonheur n'est pas absolu, car il serait irréel et stupide, et au contraire il tire tout son prix d'être en péril. Ce bonheur, cette grâce, toute pleine *et illuminante qu'elle soit, elle est liée à un destin. Destin d'une prestigieuse levée de poésie lyrique, destin de l'un de ces poètes, destin d'un peuple, et tout cela devenu interruption, inachèvement. Voilà ce qui est dit, confessé, proclamé, non seulement dans l'œuvre lyrique de Lorca, mais dans son œuvre dramatique dont l'un des thèmes principaux, sinon le principal, est le célibat, le célibat mélancolique, désespéré de la femme espagnole, de l'Espagne elle-même, la noce ensanglantée, la terre stérile, l'enfantement impossible. Et pourtant l'Espagne est maternelle et s'est maintes fois reconnue dans la figure de la mère, fût-elle vierge comme la Mère sainte Thérèse ; et l'un des thèmes obsédants d'Unamuno est celui de l'engendrement, lui qui était si fier de ses huit enfants et n'a cessé de jouer de la dialectique d'une Espagne tout ensemble sa mère qui le créait et sa fille qu'il créait. Mais en fait toute création demeure vaine, le peuple espagnol souffre et s'efforce sans parvenir à sa réalisation, sans parvenir à se créer ses lois, ses institutions, son régime, sans jamais accéder à l'histoire, et se retrouve à tout coup condamné à la tragédie.*

Ainsi en est-il de la poésie de Federico Garcia Lorca. Heureuse, géniale, miraculeuse, éminemment gracieuse, *elle est aussi tragique. Et c'est là sans doute la raison profonde de son universel succès. Ses pièces sont fascinantes parce qu'elles sont, non seulement tragiques, mais la tragédie même, l'*actus tragicus, *l'*auto sacramental, *la représentation, non point d'une circonstance particulière et de ses contingentes conséquences, mais de la Fatalité elle-même et de l'inexorable accomplissement de sa menace : elles sont une algèbre de la Fatalité. Et la moindre des poésies lyriques de Federico Garcia Lorca ou tel moment de celles-ci qui se réduit à un cri, à un soupir, à l'incantatoire évocation d'une chose, nuit, lune, rivière, cheval, femme,* *cloche, olive, possèdent la même vertu. Laquelle est si puissante que même à travers la traduction (et il faut dire que les traductions françaises ici réunies sont toutes des réussites extraordinaires, fruit de ferveurs diverses, mais également au-dessus de tout éloge) on perçoit le son et la chanson, le ton, le tour, l'évidence du langage original, sa vérité espagnole, sa vérité populaire. Et du même coup se laissent deviner, inhérente au délice, poignante, obscure, terrible, la présence de la passion et, imminente, l'effusion du sang.*

Jean Cassou

Chansons

(1921-1924)

Traduit par André Belamich.

*A Pedro Salinas, Jorge Guillén
et Melchor Fernandez Almagro.*

Théories

CHANSON DES SEPT DEMOISELLES

(Théorie de l'arc-en-ciel.)

Chantent les sept
demoiselles.

(L'arc sur le ciel
gamme du couchant.)

Une âme en sept voix
les sept demoiselles.

(Dans l'air blanc
sept oiseaux géants.)

Meurent les sept
demoiselles.

(Pourquoi n'étaient-elles
pas neuf... ou bien vingt?)

Nul ne peut les voir
car l'eau les entraîne.

NOCTURNE SCHÉMATIQUE

Fenouil, serpent et jonc.
Arôme, sillage et pénombre.
Air, terre et solitude.

(L'échelle atteint à la lune.)

LA CHANSON DU COLLÉGIEN

Samedi.
Porte de jardin.

Dimanche.
Jour gris.
Gris.

Samedi.
Voûtes bleues.
Brise.

Dimanche.
Mer et rivage.
Termes.

Samedi.
Semence
qui frémit.

Dimanche.
(Notre amour devient
tout jaune.)

LE CAILLOU VEUT ÊTRE LUMIÈRE

Le caillou veut être lumière.
Il fait luire en l'obscurité
des fils de phosphore et de lune.
Que veut-il ? se dit la lumière,
car dans ses limites d'opale
elle se retrouve elle-même
et repart.

LE MANÈGE

A José Bergamin.

Les jours de fête
tournent en rond.
Le manège les amène
et les remporte.

Bleus la Fête-Dieu
blancs à la Noël.

Les jours perdent comme
les couleuvres leur peau ancienne
à la seule exception
des jours de fête.

Ces jours sont pareils
à nos vieilles mères.
Leurs soirs ont de longues traînes
de moire avec des paillettes.

Bleus la Fête-Dieu
blancs à la Noël.

Fixé à un astre
tourne le manège.
Tulipe des cinq
continents terrestres.

Sur leurs petits chevaux
déguisés en panthères
les enfants mangent la lune
comme si c'était une prune.

Rage, rage, Marco Polo!
Dans leur fantastique ronde
les enfants voient des pays
encore inconnus au monde.

Bleus la Fête-Dieu
blancs à la Noël.

BALANCE

La nuit toujours paisible.
Le jour part et arrive.

La nuit morte et lointaine.
Le jour n'a plus qu'une aile.

La nuit sur miroirs plans
et le jour sous le vent.

CHANSON AVEC MOUVEMENT

Hier

(Étoiles
bleues.)

Demain

(Petites étoiles
blanches.)

Aujourd'hui

(Songe fleur endormie
dans le vallon de la jupe.)

Hier

(Étoiles
de feu.)

Demain

(Étoiles
violettes.)

Aujourd'hui

(Ce cœur, mon Dieu,
ce cœur qui bondit !)

Hier

(Souvenir
d'étoiles.)

Demain

(Étoiles voilées.)

Aujourd'hui...

(Demain !)

Aurais-je le mal
de mer sur la barque ?

Oh, les ponts d'aujourd'hui
sur les chemins de l'eau !

PROVERBE

Mars
en volant passe.

Janvier très haut vient derrière.

Janvier
qui suit dans la nuit du ciel.

En bas, mars, instant fugace.

Janvier
pour mes yeux usés.

Mars
pour mes fraîches mains.

FRISE

A Gustavo Duran.

TERRE

Les filles de la brise
passent en longues traînes.

CIEL

Les jouvenceaux de l'air
sautent dessus la lune.

CHASSEUR

Haute pinède!
Quatre colombes s'élèvent dans l'air.

Quatre colombes
sont revenues.
A leurs quatre ombres
une blessure.

Basse pinède!
Quatre colombes gisent à terre.

FABLE

Licornes et cyclopes.

Yeux verts
et cornes d'or.

Au bord de la falaise
en troupeau gigantesque
ils illustrent le tain
sans vitre de la mer.

Licornes et cyclopes.

Unique prunelle
unique force.

Qui doute de l'effet
terrible de ces cornes?

Nature
masque tes fins!

AOUT

Août
confrontation
de la pêche et du sucre.
Le soleil au sein du soir
comme le noyau d'un fruit.

Le maïs conserve intact
son rire jaune et dur.

Août
les enfants mangent
pain bis et lune exquise.

ARLEQUIN

Sein rouge du soleil
et sein bleu de la lune.
Torse moitié corail
moitié argent obscur.

TROIS ARBRES ABATTUS

A Ernesto Halffter.

Ils étaient trois
(Vint le jour avec ses haches.)
Ils étaient deux
(Ailes traînantes d'argent.)
Il en reste un.
Plus rien...
(L'eau reste déserte.)

Nocturnes de la fenêtre

*A la mémoire de José de Ciria
y Escalante, poète.*

I

Haute va la lune
humble court le vent.

(Mes regards profonds
explorent le ciel.)

La lune sur l'onde
lune sous le vent.

(Mes regards étroits
explorent le sol.)

La voix de deux enfants.
Je m'élève sans peine
de la lune de l'onde
à la lune du ciel.

II

La lune a fait passer
son bras par ma croisée.

C'est un grand bras de bronze
plein de bracelets d'onde.

Sur le bleu d'un cristal
joue au fleuve mon âme.

Et les instants blessés
Par l'heure... s'écoulaient.

III

La tête à ma fenêtre
je vois en me penchant
comme veut la trancher
le couperet du vent.

A cette guillotine
invisible j'ai mis
les têtes sans regards
de tous mes vieux désirs.

Une odeur de citron
emplit l'instant immense
cependant que se fait
fleur de gaze le vent.

IV

On a trouvé aujourd'hui
dans l'étang, morte, une ondine.
Hors de l'eau elle repose
sur le sol ensevelie.

Depuis sa tête à ses cuisses
va un poisson qui l'appelle.
Le vent murmure : ma fille!
Mais nul effort ne l'éveille.

Le bassin retient défaites
les algues de ses cheveux
et ses seins gris découverts
que les rainettes émeuvent.

Dieu te garde. Allons prier
Notre-Dame des Rivières
pour la fille de l'étang
morte au-dessous des pommiers.

A ses côtés je mettrai
deux petites calebasses
qui l'aideront à flotter
sur la mer salée, hélas!

1923, Résidence des Étudiants.

Chansons pour enfants

*A la merveilleuse petite
Colomba Morla Vicuña,
qui s'endormit pieusement
le 12 août 1928.*

CHANSON CHINOISE EN EUROPE

A ma filleule Isabel Clara.

La demoiselle
à l'éventail
va sur le pont
du frais ruisseau.

Et les messieurs
en redingote
mirent le pont
sans balustrade.

La demoiselle
à l'éventail
et aux volants
cherche un mari.

Mais les messieurs
sont mariés
avec des blondes
au blanc langage.

Les grillons chantent
du côté d'ouest.
(La demoiselle
va dans le vert.)

Les grillons chantent
sous les fleurettes.

(Et les messieurs
s'en vont au Nord.)

CHANSONNETTE SÉVILLANE

A Solita Salinas.

L'aube luisait
sur les orangers.
Des abeilles d'or
recherchaient le miel.

Où peut-il être,
ce miel?

Il est dans la fleur bleue,
Isabelle,
dans la fleur
là-bas de ce romarin.

(Tabouret d'or
pour le More,
et de paillettes
pour la mauresque.)

L'aube luisait
Sur les orangers.

COQUILLAGE

A Natalita Jimenez.

On m'a offert un coquillage.

Il y chante
une mer de mappemonde
et l'eau emplit mon cœur
avec ses petits poissons
d'ombre et d'argent.

On m'a offert un coquillage.

LE LÉZARD EST TOUT EN LARMES...

*A Mademoiselle Teresita Guillén
qui joue sur son piano à six notes.*

Le lézard est tout en larmes
la lézarde est tout en larmes.

Le lézard et la lézarde
en petits tabliers blancs.

Ils ont perdu par mégarde
leur anneau de mariage.

Hélas, leur anneau de plomb
leur joli anneau de plomb!

Personne dans le grand ciel
où monte un globe d'oiseaux.

Le soleil, gros capitaine,
porte un gilet de satin.

Regardez comme ils sont vieux!
Comme ils sont vieux, les lézards!

Et comme ils pleurent, mon Dieu,
Et comme ils sont tout en larmes!

CHANSON CHANTÉE

Dans le gris
l'oiseau Griffon
a mis son habit gris
et la petite Kikiriki
a perdu son teint blanc
et sa forme aussi.

Pour entrer dans le gris
je me suis peint en gris
ah! comme je luis
dans le gris!

PAYSAGE

*A Rita, Concha, Pepe
et Carmencica.*

Par mégarde le soir
s'est habillé de froid.

Derrière les carreaux
brouillés, tous les enfants
voient un bel arbre jaune
se changer en oiseaux.

Le soir s'est allongé
le long de la rivière.
Et sur les toits frissonne
une rougeur de pomme.

CHANSON BÊTE

Maman,
je voudrais être en argent.

Mon fils,
tu auras bien froid.

Maman,
je voudrais être de l'eau.

Mon fils,
tu n'auras pas chaud.

Maman,
brode-moi sur ton oreiller.

Oui, mon fils,
sans tarder!

Andaluzas

*A Miguel Pizarro (dans l'irré-
gularité symétrique du Japon).*

CHANSON DE CAVALIER

(1860)

Sous la lune noire
des pillards de route
tes éperons sonnent...

Petit cheval noir
où emportes-tu ton cavalier mort?

... Tes durs éperons,
brigand immobile
qui perdis les brides.

Petit cheval froid
quel est ce parfum de fleur de couteau?

Sous la lune noire
la Sierra Morena
a son flanc qui saigne.

Petit cheval noir
où emportes-tu ton cavalier mort?

Là-haut, la nuit plante
à ses côtes noires
des éperons d'astres.

Petit cheval froid
quel est ce parfum de fleur de couteau?

Sous la lune noire
un cri! et la corne
d'un feu de montagne.

Petit cheval noir,
où emportes-tu ton cavalier mort?

ADELINE QUI SE PROMÈNE

Il n'est point d'orange en mer
ni à Séville d'amour.
Dis, contre le feu du jour,
veux-tu m'offrir ton ombrelle?

J'aurai le visage vert
— jus de lime et de citron —
et tes mots, petits poissons,
viendront nager alentour.

Il n'est point d'orange en mer
hélas,
ni à Séville d'amour!

RONCE AU TRONC GRIS

Ronce sauvage au tronc gris
veux-tu me donner ton fruit?

Du sang et des épines. Viens.
Aime-moi, je serai tienne.

Laisse ton fruit de vert et d'ombre
fondre sur ma langue, ô ronce.

Mon étreinte serait infinie
dans la pénombre de mes épines.

Ronce, que t'en vas-tu chercher?
L'amour que tu ne sais donner.

ALLANT AU BORD DE LA MER...

Allant au bord de la mer
compter vagues et coquilles
ma belle trouva bientôt
la rivière de Séville.

Entre cloches et lauriers
se balançaient cinq navires
ayant les rames dans l'eau
et les voiles à la brise.

Qui regarde dans la tour
caparaçonnée, là-haut ?
Cinq voix nous ont répondu
rondes comme des anneaux.

Le ciel superbe montait
le fleuve, assis sur ses rives.
Dans l'air à peine rougi
cinq bagues se balançaient.

SOIR

Ma Lucie avait-elle
les pieds dans le ruisseau?

Trois immenses peupliers
une étoile.

Le silence mordu
de grenouilles paraît
une gaze piquée
de verts grains de beauté.

Sur la rive
un arbre sec
se voit fleurir en cercles
concentriques.

Et sur l'eau mes songes s'évadent
vers une fille de Grenade.

CHANSON DE CAVALIER

Cordoue
lointaine et seule.

Lune grande, jument noire,
olives dans le bissac,
j'ai beau connaître la route
je n'atteindrai pas Cordoue.
Par la plaine, par le vent,
jument noire, lune rouge,
la mort tout là-bas me guette
depuis les tours de Cordoue.

Ah, ma jument valeureuse
quelle interminable course!
Je sais que la mort m'attend
sur le chemin de Cordoue!

Cordoue
lointaine et seule.

C'EST BIEN VRAI

Ah, qu'il me coûte de peine
à t'aimer comme je t'aime!

Amoureux, l'air me fait mal,
mon cœur
et mon chapeau même.

Qui donc voudra m'acheter
ce galon tressé de soie
cette tristesse de fil
blanc à faire des mouchoirs?

Ah, qu'il me coûte de peine
à t'aimer comme je t'aime!

ARBRISSEAU

Arbrisseau sec et vert
arbrisseau.

Elle cueille les olives
la fillette au beau visage.

Le vent, vert-galant des tours,
l'a saisie par la taille.

Passent quatre cavaliers
sur des juments andalouses
en costumes bleus et verts
avec leur cape en velours.

— La belle, viens à Cordoue.
Mais elle ne les écoute.

Passent trois torerillos
minces de taille et pimpants.
Leurs habits sont orangés
leur épée en vieil argent.

— La belle, viens à Cordoue.
Mais elle ne les écoute.

Et lorsque le soir violet
pâlit dans le jour diffus,
vint un garçon qui portait
roses et myrtes de lune.

— La belle, viens à Grenade.
Mais elle n'écoute pas.

Elle cueille les olives
la fillette au beau visage
avec le bras gris du vent
serré autour de sa taille.

Arbrisseau sec et vert
arbrisseau.

JOLI CŒUR

Joli
joli cœur
on fait chez toi brûler du thym.

Tu peux partir ou rester,
j'ai fermé ma porte à clé.

D'une clé de fin argent
attachée à un ruban.

Ce ruban porte en devise :
Mon cœur est bien loin d'ici.

Abandonne ma ruelle,
laisses-y circuler l'air!

Joli
joli cœur
on fait chez toi brûler du thym!

Trois portraits avec ombre

I. VERLAINE

La chanson
que jamais je ne dirai
s'est endormie à mes lèvres.
La chanson
que jamais je ne dirai.

Parmi les chèvrefeuilles
était un ver luisant
et la lune effleurait
l'eau d'un de ses rayons.

Et alors je rêvai
la chanson
que jamais je ne dirai.

Chanson pleine de lèvres
et de rives lointaines.

Chanson des heures longues
que je perdis dans l'ombre.

Chanson d'étoile vive
sur un jour infini.

BACCHUS

Verte rumeur intacte.
Le figuier me tend ses bras.

Comme une panthère, son ombre
guette la lyre de mon ombre.

La lune compte les chiens
se trompe et sans fin recommence.

Hier, demain, noir et vert,
tu hantes mon cercle de laurier.

Qui t'aimerait autant
que moi, le cœur changé?
... Et le figuier en criant s'avance
terrible et multiplié.

II. JUAN RAMON JIMENEZ

Dans le blanc infini,
neige, nard et saline,
se perd sa fantaisie.

Elle va sur le blanc,
silencieux tapis
de plumes de colombe.

Sans regard, immobile,
elle souffre le songe
mais frissonne en dedans.

Dans le blanc infini
quelle pure blessure
laisse sa fantaisie!

Dans le blanc infini.
Neige, nard et saline.

VÉNUS

Ainsi t'ai-je vue.

La jeune morte
sur la nacre de sa couche
nudité de brise en fleur
surgissait au jour éternel.

Le monde qui restait,
iris d'ombre et coton,
regardait à la croisée
l'écoulement sans fin des choses.

La jeune morte
creusait l'amour en son tréfonds.
Entre l'écume de ses draps
se perdait sa chevelure.

III. DEBUSSY

Mon ombre passe en silence
sur l'eau fraîche du canal.

Mon ombre en passant efface
aux grenouilles les étoiles.

L'ombre pose sur mon corps
des reflets de choses calmes.

Mon ombre passe comme un
immense insecte lilas.

Cent grillons veulent dorer
le jour des herbes sauvages.

Une clarté naît en moi
reflet venu du canal.

NARCISSE

Enfant,
Tu vas tomber dans la rivière!

      Au fond de l'eau est une rose
    et dans la rose une autre rivière.

Vois donc cet oiseau! Regarde
là-bas cet oiseau tout jaune!

        Mes yeux sont tombés
        au fond de l'eau.

Mon Dieu!
Mais il glisse, cet enfant!

      ... et au cœur de la rose moi-même.

Lorsqu'il se perdit dans l'eau
je compris. Je n'explique pas.

Jeux

*Dédiés à la tête de Luis Buñuel.
En gros plan.*

RIVERAINES
(Avec accompagnement de cloches.)

On dit que tu as une
(Balalin!)
tête de pleine lune.
(Balalan!)
Que de cloches, tu entends?
(Balalin!)
Elles ne me lâchent pas.
(Balalan!)
Mais tes yeux... ah!
(Balalin!)
... pardon, tes œillères...
(Balalan!)
et ce rire d'or
(Balalin!)
et cette... rien à faire, cette...
(Balalan!)

A sa dure crinoline
cognaient les coups de cloche.

ô ton charme secret... ton...

(Balalin
lin
lin
lin...)

oh, pardon!

A IRÈNE GARCIA
(domestique)

Dans le bosquet
dansent les jeunes peupliers
l'un avec l'autre
et l'arbrisseau
avec ses quatre brins de feuilles
danse comme eux.

Irène!
Bientôt viendront les pluies
et les neiges.
Va danser sur le vert.

Sur le vert qui verdoie
moi j'irai avec toi.

Ah, comme l'eau court vite!
Ah, mon cœur!

Dans le bosquet
dansent les jeunes peupliers
l'un avec l'autre
et l'arbrisseau
avec ses quatre brins de feuilles
danse comme eux.

A L'OREILLE D'UNE JEUNE FILLE

Je n'ai rien voulu
rien voulu te dire.

J'ai vu dans tes yeux
deux jeunes arbres fous
de brise, de rire et d'or,
qui remuaient.

Je n'ai rien voulu
rien voulu te dire.

LES GENS S'EN ALLAIENT...

Les gens s'en allaient
et l'automne venait.
Les gens
s'en allaient au vert
avec leurs coqs
et leur guitare en fête
par le royaume
des graines.
Le fleuve songeait,
coulait la fontaine.
Bondis
ô cœur brûlant!

Les gens
s'en allaient au vert.
Et l'automne venait
tout cuivré d'étoiles
avec ses oiseaux mornes
ses ondes concentriques.
Arrête-toi
cœur de cire!

Les gens s'en allaient
et l'automne venait.

CHANSON DU « MARIQUITA [1] »

Le *mariquita* se coiffe
dans son peignoir de satin.

On échange des sourires
chez les voisins aux fenêtres.

Le *mariquita* compose
une à une ses bouclettes.

La cour bruit de perroquets
de jets d'eau et de planètes.

Le *mariquita* se pare
effrontément d'un jasmin.

La nuit extravague avec
ses liserons et ses peignes.

Le tumulte de la ville
frémit, rayé comme un zèbre.

Les *mariquitas* du Sud
aux terrasses vont chanter!

1. Nom des efféminés en Espagne.

ARBRE DE CHANT

Pour Ana Maria Dali.

Le roseau, voix et geste,
de nouveau, derechef,
tremble sans espérance
sur la brise d'hier.

La fille en soupirant
Le voulait attraper
mais arrivait toujours
une minute après.

Ah, soleil, lune, lune!
Une minute après.
Soixante fleurs pâlies
s'enroulaient à ses pieds.

Vois comme il se balance
de nouveau, derechef,
nu de fleurs et de branches
dans la brise d'hier.

ORANGE ET CITRON

Orange et citron.

Bien triste est celle
qu'amour tourmente!

Citron et orange.

Bien triste es-tu
fillette blanche!

Citron.

(Comme brillait
le soleil blond.)

Orange.

(Sur les cailloux
de l'onde.)

LA RUE DES MUETS

Derrière les vitres immobiles
les jeunes filles jouent avec leurs rires.

> (Dans les pianos vides
> araignées acrobatiques.)

Les jeunes filles parlent de leurs fiancés
en agitant leurs tresses nouées.

> (Monde de l'éventail :
> la main et le mouchoir.)

Les galants en réplique prodiguent
des ailes et des fleurs avec leurs capes noires.

Chansons de lune

A José F. Montesinos.

LA LUNE QUI PARAIT

Quand se montre la lune
les carillons s'effacent
et luisent des sentiers
impénétrables.

Quand se montre la lune
la mer couvre la terre
et notre cœur dérive,
île dans l'infini.

Nul ne mange d'oranges
sous le grand clair de lune.
Il faut pourtant manger
des fruits verts et glacés.

Quand se montre la lune
aux cent têtes égales
les piécettes d'argent
sanglotent dans la bourse.

DEUX LUNES DU SOIR

I

A Laurita, amie de ma sœur.

La lune est morte, morte
mais ressuscite au printemps.

Lorsqu'au front des peupliers
écumera le vent du Sud.

Lorsque nos cœurs livreront
leur récolte de soupirs.

Lorsque les toits se coifferont
de leurs petits chapeaux d'herbe.

La lune est morte, morte
mais ressuscite au printemps.

A Isabelita, ma sœur.

Le soir chantonne
une berceuse aux oranges.

Isabelita chante :
La terre est une orange.

La lune dit en pleurant :
Je voudrais être une orange.

C'est impossible, ma fille,
quand tu te peindrais en rose !
C'est bien dommage !
Pas même un petit citron.

LUNDI, MERCREDI, VENDREDI

J'étais.
Je fus
mais je ne suis.

J'étais...
(O gorge merveilleuse
du cyprès et de l'ombre!
Angle de pleine lune.
Angle de lune seule.)

Je fus...
La lune pour badiner
veut passer pour une rose.
(Dans une cape de vent
mon amour à l'eau s'est jeté.)

Mais je ne suis...
(Devant un carreau brisé
je couds mes haillons lyriques.)

MORT AU PETIT MATIN

Nuit aux quatre lunes
avec un seul arbre,
une seule ombre,
un seul oiseau.

Je cherche sur mon corps
la chaleur de tes lèvres.
La source baise le vent
sans le toucher.

J'ai le Non que tu m'offris
dans la paume de ma main
comme un citron de cire
presque blanc.

Nuit aux quatre lunes
avec un seul arbre.
A la pointe d'une aiguille
tourne, tourne mon amour!

PREMIER ANNIVERSAIRE

Elle circule en mon front.
O le regret ancien!

A quoi me sert, dites-moi,
le papier, l'encre ou les vers?

D'ici ta chair me paraît
un jonc frais, un rouge lys.

O brune du clair de lune,
que fais-tu de mon désir?

DEUXIÈME ANNIVERSAIRE

La lune pique la mer
d'une longue corne claire.

Licorne grise et verte
frémissante et extatique.

Le ciel flotte sur les airs,
immense fleur de lotus.

(O toi seule, passant par
l'ultime salle des nuits!)

FLEUR

A Colin Hackforth.

Le magnifique saule
de la pluie pleurait.

O la lune ronde
sur les branches blanches!

Éros avec canne
(1925)

A Pépin Bello.

FRAYEUR DANS LA SALLE A MANGER

Tu étais rose.
Tu devins toute blême.

Quelle intention vis-tu en ma main
qui presque te menaçait?

Je voulais les pommes vertes
et non les pommes roses...

Toute blême...

(Grue endormie le soir
pose à terre l'autre patte.)

LUCIA MARTINEZ

Lucia Martinez.
Ombrage de satin rouge.

Tes cuisses comme le soir
vont de la lumière à l'ombre.
Le noir le plus secret du jais
obscurcit tes magnolias.
Me voici, Lucia Martinez.
Je viens dévorer ta bouche
et te traîner par les cheveux
dans une aube de coquillages.

Je le veux et je le peux,
ombrage de satin rouge.

LA VIEILLE FILLE A LA MESSE

Sous le Moïse de l'encens,
assoupie.

Des yeux de taureau te guettent.
Ton chapelet tombe en pluie.

Dans ta toilette de soie sombre
ne bouge point, Virginie.

Offre les noirs melons de tes seins
à la rumeur de l'office.

INTÉRIEUR

Je ne veux être poète
ni galant.
Blancheur des draps où tu défailles!

Tu ne connais le rêve
ni la splendeur du jour.
Comme les seiches
dans l'encre des parfums ta nudité aveugle,
Carmen.

NU

Sous le laurier-rose sans lune
tu étais laide, toute nue.

Ta chair quêtait sur ma carte
le jaune de l'Espagne.

Car tu étais laide, Française,
sous le laurier-rose amer.

Rouge et verte je te lançai
la cape de mon talent.

Verte et rouge, rouge et verte.
Ici, nous sommes différents!

SÉRÉNADE

(Hommage à Lope de Vega.)

Sur les bords de la rivière
voyez la nuit qui se baigne
et sur les seins de Lolita
meurent d'amour les bouquets.

Meurent d'amour les bouquets.

La nuit nue chante à voix basse
sur les ponts du mois de mars.
Lolita au bain se pare
dans l'eau saline et le nard.

Meurent d'amour les bouquets.

La nuit d'anis et d'argent
luit sur les toits de la ville.
Argent des eaux miroitantes.
Anis de tes cuisses blanches.

Meurent d'amour les bouquets.

A MALAGA

Somptueuse Leonarda.
Chair pontificale en robe blanche
aux balustrades de la Villa Leonarda.
Exposée aux tramways et aux bateaux.
Des torses noirs de baigneurs assombrissent
la rive de la mer. En oscillant
— conque et lotus à la fois —
arrive ta croupe
de Cérès en rhétorique de marbre.

Outremonde

A Manuel Angeles Ortiz.

SCÈNE

Hautes tours.
Vastes fleuves.

FÉE

Prends l'anneau de mariage
que portèrent tes aïeux.
Cent mains, sous leur poids de terre
regrettent d'en être veuves.

MOI

Je vais sentir dans mes mains
une immense fleur de doigts
le symbole de l'anneau.
Je n'en veux pas.
Hautes tours.
Vastes fleuves.

NUIT ET MALAISE

Guêpier.
Dans tes arbres obscurs.
Nuit au ciel balbutiant
où la brise bégaie.
Trois ivrognes éternisent
leurs gestes de deuil et de vin.
Les astres de plomb pivotent
sur un pied.
            Guêpier.
Dans tes arbres obscurs.

Douleur aux tempes serrées
de guirlandes de minutes.
Et ton silence? Les trois
ivrognes chantent tout nus.
Point festonné sur soie vierge,
ta chanson.
            Guêpier.
Pi-er pi-er pi-er pi-er
            Guêpier.

L'ENFANT MUET

L'enfant cherche sa voix.
(C'est le roi des grillons qui l'a.)
Dans une goutte d'eau
cherchait sa voix l'enfant.

Je n'en veux point pour parler.
Je m'en ferai une bague
que portera mon silence
autour de son petit doigt.

Dans une goutte d'eau
cherchait sa voix l'enfant.

(La voix prisonnière au loin
mettait un habit de grillon.)

L'ENFANT FOU

Je disais : « Le soir ».
Ce n'était pas ça.
Le soir était autre chose...
Il s'était en allé.

(Et la lumière haussait
les épaules comme une fillette.)

« Le soir. » Mais c'est inutile !
Celui-ci est faux, il a
une demi-lune de plomb.
L'autre ne viendra jamais.

(Et la lumière comme tous la voient
jouait à la statue avec l'enfant fou.)

L'autre était tout petit
et mangeait des grenades.
Celui-ci est gros et vert, je ne peux
le prendre dans mes bras ni l'habiller.
Ne viendra-t-il pas ? Comment était-il ?

(La lumière en partant, pour rire,
sépara l'enfant de son ombre.)

FIANÇAILLES

Jetez cet anneau
dans l'eau.

(L'ombre appuie ses doigts
sur mon dos.)

Jetez cet anneau. J'ai
plus de cent ans. Silence!

Ne me demandez rien!

Jetez cet anneau
dans l'eau.

ADIEU

Si je meurs
laissez le balcon ouvert.

L'enfant mange des oranges.
(De mon balcon je le vois.)

Le moissonneur fauche le blé.
(De mon balcon je l'entends.)

Si je meurs
laissez le balcon ouvert!

SUICIDE

(Peut-être parce que tu ignorais la géométrie.)

Le jeune homme perdait mémoire de lui-même.
Il était dix heures du matin.

Son cœur peu à peu s'emplissait
de fleurs de chiffon et d'ailes brisées.

Il nota qu'il ne lui restait
plus qu'une parole aux lèvres.

Otant les gants, il vit tomber
de ses mains une cendre fine.

Du balcon se voyait une tour.
Il se sentit balcon et tour.

Il crut voir que le fixait
la montre prise dans son boîtier.

Il vit son ombre étendue et calme
sur le blanc divan de soie.

Le jeune homme, géométrique et roide,
d'un coup de hache brisa le miroir.

A ce geste un grand jet d'ombre
inonda la chimérique alcôve.

Amour

(Avec ailes et flèches.)

PETIT AIR DU PREMIER DÉSIR

Dans la matinée verte
je voulais être un cœur.
Un cœur.

Et dans la soirée mûre
je voulais être un rossignol.
Rossignol.

(Mon âme,
rougis comme l'orange.
Mon âme,
rougis comme l'amour.)

Dans la matinée vive
je voulais être moi.
Un cœur.

Et dans le soir tombé
je voulais être ma voix.
Rossignol.

Mon âme,
rougis comme l'orange.
Mon âme,
rougis comme l'amour!

AU LYCÉE ET A L'UNIVERSITÉ

La première fois
je ne te reconnus pas.
La deuxième, si.

Dis-moi,
l'air te l'apprend-il ?
Petit matin froid
je devenais triste
lorsque je fus pris
d'une envie de rire.
Je ne te reconnus pas.
Toi si.
Je te reconnus.
Toi non.
Voici qu'entre nous
s'étire impassible

un mois comme un
paravent de jours gris.

La première fois
je ne te reconnus pas.
La deuxième, si.

PETIT MADRIGAL

Quatre grenadiers
sont dans ton verger.

(Prends mon cœur
tout neuf.)
Quatre cyprès
y seront plantés.

(Prends mon cœur
si vieux.)

Soleil et lune.
Après...
ni cœur
ni verger!

ÉCHO

Voici que s'ouvre
la fleur de l'aurore.

(Te souviens-tu
de ce fond de soir ?)

Le nard de la lune
épand son parfum froid.

(Te souviens-tu
de ce regard d'août ?)

IDYLLE

A Enrique Duran.

Tu voulais que je te dise
le secret du renouveau.
Mais je garde le secret
tout autant que le sapin.

Arbre dont les mille doigts
indiquent mille chemins.

Je ne te dirai jamais, mon amour,
pourquoi si lentement le fleuve coule.

Mais je mettrai en ma voix d'eau dormante
le ciel cendré de tes regards.

Tourne autour de moi, ma brune,
et prends bien garde à mes feuilles.
Tourne encore, tourne toujours
jouant à la noria de l'amour.

Quand je le voudrais, je ne puis te dire,
hélas, le secret du renouveau.

NARCISSE

Narcisse.
Ton odeur.
Et le fond de l'onde.

Je veux rester près de toi.
Fleur de l'amour.
Narcisse.

Dans tes yeux blancs passent l'onde
et des poissons qui sommeillent.
Des oiseaux, des papillons
japonisent dans les miens.

Tout petit près de moi grand.
Fleur de l'amour.
Narcisse.

Les grenouilles — combien vives! —
ne veulent laisser tranquille
le miroir sur quoi se mirent
ton délire et mon délire.

Narcisse.
Ma douleur.
Et ma douleur même.

GRENADE EN 1850

Depuis ma chambre
j'entends le jet d'eau.

Un doigt de la treille
un rais de soleil
désignent le lieu
où est mon cœur.

Sur la brise d'août
s'en vont les nuées.
Au cœur du jet d'eau, je rêve
que je suis éveillé.

PRÉLUDE

Les hauts peupliers s'en vont
mais ils laissent leur reflet.

Les hauts peupliers s'en vont
mais ils nous laissent le vent.

Mais ils ont laissé flottants
sur les fleuves leurs échos.

Le monde des vers luisants
a envahi ma mémoire

tandis que me pousse un cœur
minuscule entre les doigts.

SUR LE VERT DU CIEL...

Sur le vert du ciel
une étoile verte
que peut-elle faire, mon amour
ah, sinon se perdre?

Les tours qui se noient
dans le brouillard froid
comment pourraient-elles
nous voir des fenêtres?

Cent étoiles vertes
sur le vert du ciel
ne voient point cent tours
blanches dans la neige.

Le chagrin que j'ai,
pour qu'il se ranime
je veux le parer
de rouges sourires.

SONNET

Spectre d'argent aux franges qui frémissent
la brise de la nuit en soupirant
rouvre ma vieille plaie de sa main grise
et s'éloigne : je reste pantelant.

Douleur d'amour d'où rejaillit la vie,
puits éternel de lumière et de sang,
retraite où Philomèle muette et triste
trouve son nid, ses bois et son tourment.

Ah, quelle douce rumeur dans ma tête!
Je m'étendrai près de la fleur naïve
où flottera sans âme ta beauté,

et là, tandis que blondira l'eau vive,
mon sang se répandra par la jonchaie
humide et odorante de la rive.

Chansons pour finir

A Rafael Alberti.

D'UNE AUTRE FAÇON

A la plaine du soir le feu de joie
met des ramures de cerf en furie.
Tout le vallon repose. Sur son dos
caracole un léger zéphyr.

L'air s'affine en cristal sous la fumée
comme un œil de chat jaune et triste.
Moi dans mes yeux je me promène
par le feuillage qui s'en va le long des rives.

Il atteint mille choses essentielles
— ritournelles de ritournelles —
Parmi l'arrière-soir peuplé de joncs
« Federico », curieux que j'aie ce nom!

CHANSON DE NOVEMBRE ET D'AVRIL

Le ciel nuageux
me fait des yeux blancs.

Pour leur rendre vie
j'en approche une fleur
jaune vif.

Je ne puis les troubler.
Ils restent blancs, glacés.

(A mes épaules vole
pleine, mon âme d'or.)

Mais le ciel d'avril
me fait des yeux de saphir.

Pour leur donner âme, je penche
près d'eux une rose blanche.

Je ne puis mêler
le blanc au saphir.

(A mes épaules voltige
aveugle, mon âme impassible.)

ONDE, OU T'EN VAS-TU?...

Onde, où t'en vas-tu?

Je m'écoule en riant
jusqu'au bord de la mer.

Mer, où t'en vas-tu?

Remontant le cours d'eau je cherche
la fontaine où me reposer.

Que fais-tu, toi, peuplier?

Je ne veux rien te dire.
Je ne puis que trembler!

Où lancer mes désirs
par le fleuve et la mer?

(Quatre oiseaux se sont posés
sans but sur le haut peuplier.)

LE MIROIR TROMPEUR

Verte branche vierge
de rythme et d'oiseau.

Écho de sanglot
sans douleur ni lèvres.
Homme et forêt.

Je pleure
face aux flots amers
et dans mes prunelles
il chante deux mers!

CHANSON INUTILE

Rose future et veine contenue,
améthyste d'hier et brise d'aujourd'hui
je veux les oublier!

Homme et poisson en leur mitan sous des choses
flottantes
espérant sur la chaise et dans l'algue leur nuit,
je veux les oublier!

Moi.
Rien que moi!
Ouvrageant le plateau
où n'ira point ma tête.
Rien que moi!

VERGER DE MARS

Mon pommier
abrite déjà de l'ombre et des ailes.

De la lune au vent
quel bond fait mon rêve!

Mon pommier
livre ses bras au vert.

Depuis mars, comme je vois
le front neigeux de janvier!

Mon pommier...
(Brise à terre.)

Mon pommier...
(Profond ciel.)

DEUX MARINS AU BORD DE L'EAU

A Joaquin Amigo.

I

Il rapportait en son cœur
un poisson des Mers de Chine.

Parfois on le voit passer
minuscule dans ses yeux.

Il oublie la marine
et les bars et les oranges.

Il regarde l'eau.

II

D'une langue de savon
il lava ses mots et se tut.

Monde uni, mer frisée
cent étoiles, son navire.

Il a vu les balcons du Pape
et les seins dorés des Cubaines.

Il regarde l'eau.

ANGOISSE DE STATUE

Rumeur.
Dût-il ne rester que la rumeur.

Arôme.
Dût-il ne rester que l'arôme.

Mais arrache-moi le souvenir
et la couleur des heures anciennes.

Douleur.
Face à la magique et vive douleur.
Bataille.
Dans l'authentique et impure bataille.

Mais éloigne ces gens invisibles
qui rôdent sans cesse autour de moi!

CHANSON DE L'ORANGER SEC

A Carmen Morales.

Bûcheron.
Viens abattre mon ombre
et délivre-moi du supplice
de me voir sans oranges.

Pourquoi suis-je né entre des miroirs?
Le jour tourne autour de moi
et la nuit me répète
avec toutes ses étoiles.

Je veux vivre sans me voir.
Les fourmis et les chardons
je rêverai que ce sont
mes feuilles et mes oiseaux.

Bûcheron.
Viens abattre mon ombre
et délivre-moi du supplice
de me voir sans oranges.

117

CHANSON DU JOUR QUI S'EN VA

Ah, qu'il me coûte de peine
à te laisser partir, ô jour!
Tu t'en vas rempli de moi
et reviens sans me connaître.
Ah, qu'il me coûte de peine
à laisser sur la poitrine
les possibles réalités
de minutes impossibles!

Vers le soir un Persée
vient limer tes chaînes
et tu t'enfuis sur les monts
où tu te blesses les pieds.
Rien ne peut te séduire,
ni mon corps ni mes larmes
ni les fleuves sur lesquels
tu fais ta sieste dorée.

De l'Orient à l'Occident
je porte ta lumière ronde,
ta grande lumière que soutient
mon âme à bout de tension.
De l'Orient à l'Occident
qu'il me coûte de peine
à te porter avec tes oiseaux
et tes grands bras de vent!

Poème du cante jondo

Traduit par Pierre Darmangeat.

Petite ballade des trois rivières

Le fleuve Guadalquivir
va parmi oranges et olives.
Les deux rivières de Grenade
descendent de la neige au blé.

Hélas, amour
qui s'en fut et ne vint!

Le fleuve Guadalquivir
a la barbe grenat.
Des rivières de Grenade,
l'une pleure et l'autre saigne.

Hélas, amour
qui s'en fut dans l'air!

Pour les bateaux à voiles
Séville a un chemin;
mais dans l'eau de Grenade
rament seuls les soupirs.

Hélas, amour
qui s'en fut et ne vint!

Guadalquivir, haute tour
et vent dans les orangers.
Darro et Genil, tourelles
mortes sur les étangs.

Hélas, amour
qui s'en fut dans l'air !

Qui dira que l'eau emporte
un feu follet de cris!

Hélas, amour
qui s'en fut et ne vint !

Porte la fleur d'orange, porte l'olive,
Andalousie, à tes mers.

Hélas, amour
qui s'en fut dans l'air !

Poème de la séguidille gitane

PAYSAGE

La campagne
d'oliviers
s'ouvre et se ferme
comme un éventail.
Sur l'olivette,
un ciel écroulé
et une pluie obscure
d'étoiles froides.
Au bord de la rivière
tremblent jonc et pénombre.
L'air gris se froisse.
Les oliviers
sont lourds
de cris.
Une troupe
d'oiseaux captifs,
qui remuent leurs très longues
queues dans l'obscurité.

LA GUITARE

Commence le pleur
de la guitare.
De la prime aube
les coupes se brisent.
Commence le pleur
de la guitare.
Il est inutile
de la faire taire.
Il est impossible
de la faire taire.
C'est un pleur monotone,
comme le pleur de l'eau,
comme le pleur du vent
sur la neige tombée.
Il est impossible
de la faire taire.
Elle pleure sur des choses
lointaines.
Sable du Sud brûlant
qui veut de blancs camélias.
Elle pleure la flèche sans but,
le soir sans lendemain,
et le premier oiseau mort
sur la branche.
O guitare!
O cœur à mort blessé
par cinq épées.

LE CRI

L'ellipse d'un cri
va de montagne
à montagne.

De l'oliveraie,
ce doit être un arc-en-ciel noir
sur la nuit bleue.

Aïe!

Comme l'archet d'un violon,
le cri a fait vibrer
les longues cordes du vent.

Aïe!

(Les gens qui vivent dans les grottes
sortent leurs quinquets.)

Aïe!

LE SILENCE

Entends, mon fils, le silence.
C'est un silence ondulé,
un silence
où glissent échos et vallées
et qui fait s'incliner les fronts
vers le sol.

PASSAGE DE LA SÉGUIDILLE

Parmi des papillons noirs,
va une fille brune
à côté d'un blanc serpent
de brouillard.

Terre de lumière,
ciel de terre.

Elle est enchaînée au frémissement
d'un rythme qui jamais n'arrive;
elle a un cœur d'argent
et un poignard dans la main droite.

Où vas-tu, séguidille,
avec un rythme sans tête?
Quelle lune recueillera
ta douleur de chaux et de laurier-rose?

Terre de lumière,
ciel de terre.

APRÈS LE PASSAGE

Les enfants regardent
un point éloigné.

Les chaleils s'éteignent.
Des jeunes filles aveugles
interrogent la lune,
et dans l'air s'élèvent
des spirales de pleurs.

Les montagnes regardent
un point éloigné.

ET APRÈS

Les labyrinthes
que crée le temps
s'évanouissent.

(Seul reste •
le désert.)

Le cœur,
fontaine du désir,
s'évanouit.

(Seul reste
le désert.)

L'illusion de l'aurore
et les baisers,
s'évanouissent.

Seul reste
le désert.
Un désert
onduleux.

Poème de la Solea

Terre sèche,
terre quiète
aux nuits
immenses.

(Vent dans l'olivette,
vent dans la montagne.)

Terre
vieille,
chaleil
et douleur.
Terre
aux profondes citernes.
Terre
où la mort est sans yeux,
où volent des flèches.

(Vent par les chemins.
Brise dans les peupliers.)

VILLAGE

Sur le mont pelé
un calvaire.
Eau claire
et oliviers centenaires.
Dans les ruelles,
des hommes embossés,
et sur les tours
des girouettes qui tournent.
Qui éternellement
tournent.
O village perdu
dans l'Andalousie éplorée!

POIGNARD

Le poignard
entre dans le cœur,
comme un soc de charrue
dans le désert.

Non.
Ne le cloue pas dans ma chair.
Non.

Le poignard,
comme un rais de soleil,
incendie les terribles
profondeurs.

Non.
Ne le cloue pas dans ma chair.
Non.

CARREFOUR

Vent de l'Est;
un réverbère
et le poignard
dans le cœur.
La rue vibre
comme une corde
tendue,
elle vibre
comme une mouche énorme.
De toutes parts
je
vois le poignard
dans le cœur.

AÏE!

Le cri laisse dans le vent
une ombre de cyprès.

(Laissez-moi dans ce champ,
pleurer.)

Tout s'est brisé dans le monde.
Il ne reste que le silence.

(Laissez-moi dans ce champ,
pleurer.)

L'horizon sans lumière
est mordu de brasiers.

(Je vous ai déjà dit de me laisser
dans ce champ,
pleurer.)

SURPRISE

Mort il resta dans la rue,
un poignard dans la poitrine.
Nul ne le connaissait.
Comme tremblait le réverbère!
Mère!
Comme tremblait le réverbère
de la rue!
C'était à l'aube. Nul
ne put paraître à ses yeux
ouverts dans l'air dur.
Mort, oui mort il resta dans la rue,
et un poignard dans la poitrine,
et nul, nul ne le connaissait.

LA SOLEA

Vêtue de voiles noirs
elle pense que le monde est bien petit
et que le cœur est immense.

Vêtue de voiles noirs.

Elle pense que le tendre soupir
et le cri, disparaissent
dans le courant du vent.

Vêtue de voiles noirs.

On a laissé le balcon ouvert,
et à l'aube, par le balcon
tout le ciel s'est jeté.

Aïe ! Aaah !...
Vêtue, oui, de voiles noirs !

GROTTE

De la grotte il sort
de longs sanglots.

(Le violet
sur le rouge.)

Le gitan évoque
de lointains pays.

(Hautes tours et hommes
mystérieux.)

Dans sa voix entrecoupée
vont ses yeux.

(Le noir
sur le rouge.)

Et la grotte, blanc-de-chaux,
tremble dans l'or.

(Le blanc
sur le rouge.)

RENCONTRE

Ni toi ni moi ne sommes
disposés
à nous rencontrer.
Toi... pour ce que tu sais.
Je l'ai tant aimée!
Suis cette piste.
Mes mains
sont percées
par les clous.
Ne vois-tu pas comme
je perds mon sang?
Ne regarde jamais derrière,
va doucement
et prie comme moi
saint Gaétan,
car ni toi ni moi ne sommes
disposés
à nous rencontrer.

AUBE

Cloches de Cordoue
dans le petit jour.
Cloches de l'aube
à Grenade.
Toutes les filles vous entendent,
qui pleurent la tendre
solea endeuillée.
Les jeunes filles
de la basse
et de la haute Andalousie.
Les filles d'Espagne,
au pied menu,
aux jupes frémissantes,
qui ont mis des lumières
à tous les carrefours.
Oh! cloches de Cordoue
dans le petit jour,
et vous, cloches de l'aube
à Grenade!

Poème de la Saeta

ARCHERS

Les sombres archers
s'approchent de Séville.

Guadalquivir ouvert.

Larges chapeaux gris,
longues capes lentes.

Ah, Guadalquivir!

Ils viennent des lointains
pays de la détresse.

Guadalquivir ouvert.

Et ils vont à un labyrinthe.
Amour, cristal et pierre.

Ah, Guadalquivir!

NUIT

Chaleil, cierge,
lanterne et ver luisant.
La constellation
de la saeta.

Des lucarnes d'or
tremblent,
et se bercent dans l'aurore
des croix superposées.

Chaleil, cierge,
lanterne et ver luisant.

SÉVILLE

Séville est une tour
pleine de fins archers.

Séville pour blesser.
Cordoue pour y mourir.

Une ville qui épie
de longues cadences,
et qui les enroule
comme des labyrinthes.
Comme des sarments
enflammés.

Séville pour blesser !

Sous l'arche du ciel,
sur sa plaine limpide,
elle décoche la constante
flèche de son fleuve.

Cordoue pour y mourir.

Et, folle d'horizons,
elle mêle à son vin
l'amertume de Don Juan,
la perfection de Dionysos.

Séville pour blesser !
Toujours Séville pour blesser !

PROCESSION

Par la ruelle viennent
d'étranges unicornes.
De quelle campagne,
de quel bois mythologique?
Plus près,
on dirait des astronomes.
Fantastiques Merlins
et l'Ecce Homo,
Durandart enchanté.
Roland furieux.

PASO

Vierge en vertugadin,
Vierge de la Solitude,
épanouie comme une immense
tulipe.
Sur ton bateau lumineux
tu vas
par la haute marée
de la ville,
entre de troubles saetas
et des étoiles de cristal.
Vierge en vertugadin,
tu vas
par le fleuve de la rue
jusqu'à la mer!

SAETA

Christ brun
changé
de lys de Judée
en œillet d'Espagne.

Voyez-le qui s'avance !

D'Espagne.
Ciel limpide et obscur,
terre grillée,
fossés où coule,
très lentement, l'eau.
Christ brun,
aux longs cheveux brûlés,
aux pommettes saillantes
et aux pupilles blanches.

Voyez-le qui s'en va !

BALCON

La Lola
chante des saetas.
Les toreros
l'entourent,
et le barbier,
devant sa porte,
suit le rythme
avec la tête.
Entre le basilic
et la fleur de menthe,
la Lola chante
des saetas.
Cette Lola
qui se mirait
dans le bassin.

PETIT JOUR

Mais comme l'amour
ceux qui lancent la saeta
sont aveugles.
Sur la nuit verte,
les saetas
laissent des traces d'iris
chaud.
La quille de la lune
fend des nuées violettes
et les carquois
s'emplissent de rosée.
Ah! mais comme l'amour
ceux qui lancent la saeta
sont aveugles!

Graphique de la Petenera

CLOCHE

Bourdon

Dans la tour
jaune,
une cloche sonne le glas.

Sur le vent
jaune,
s'épanouissent les sons de cloche.

Dans la tour
jaune,
s'arrête la cloche.

Le vent dans la poussière
sculpte des proues d'argent.

CHEMIN

Cent cavaliers en deuil,
où s'en vont-ils,
par le ciel gisant
de l'orangeraie?
Ni à Cordoue ni à Séville
n'arriveront.
Ni à Grenade qui soupire
après la mer.
Ces chevaux somnolents
les mèneront
au labyrinthe du calvaire
où tremble le *cantar*.
Percés de leurs sept plaintes,
où s'en vont-ils,
les cavaliers andalous
de l'orangeraie?

LES SIX CORDES

La guitare
fait pleurer les songes.
Le sanglot des âmes
perdues
s'échappe par sa bouche
ronde.

Et comme la tarentule,
elle tisse une grande étoile
pour chasser les soupirs
qui flottent dans sa noire
citerne de bois.

DANSE

Dans le jardin de la Petenera

Dans la nuit du jardin,
six gitanes
vêtues de blanc,
dansent.

Dans la nuit du jardin,
couronnées
de roses de papier
et de visnages.

Dans la nuit du jardin,
leurs dents de nacre
écrivent l'ombre
brûlée.

Et dans la nuit du jardin,
leurs ombres s'allongent
et arrivent au ciel,
violettes.

MORT DE LA PETENERA

Dans la maison blanche meurt
la perdition des hommes.

Cent poneys caracolent.
Leurs cavaliers sont morts.

Sous les frémissantes
étoiles des quinquets,
sa jupe de moire tremble
entre ses cuisses de cuivre.

Cent poneys caracolent.
Leurs cavaliers sont morts.

De longues ombres effilées
viennent de l'horizon brouillé,
et le bourdon d'une guitare
se rompt.

Cent poneys caracolent
Leurs cavaliers sont morts.

FAUSSET

Aïe, petenera gitane!
Aïe, aïe, petenera!
Ton enterrement n'eut pas de fillettes
sages.
Des fillettes qui donnent au Christ mort
leurs chevelures,
et portent de blanches mantilles
les jours de fête.
Ton enterrement fut plein de gens
sinistres.
De gens qui ont le cœur
dans la tête,
qui te suivirent en pleurant
par les ruelles.
Aïe, petenera gitane!
Aïe, aïe, petenera!

DE PROFUNDIS

Les cent amoureux
dorment pour toujours
sous la terre sèche.
L'Andalousie
a de longs chemins rouges.
Cordoue, des oliviers verts
où planter cent croix
en souvenir d'eux.
Les cent amoureux
dorment pour toujours.

CLAMEUR

Dans les tours
jaunes,
les cloches sonnent le glas.

Sur les vents
jaunes,
s'épanouissent les sons des cloches.

Par un chemin s'en va
la mort, couronnée
de fleurs d'oranger fanées.
Elle chante et chante
une chanson
sur sa viole blanche,
elle chante, chante, chante.

Dans les tours jaunes,
s'arrêtent les cloches.

Le vent dans la poussière
sculpte des proues d'argent.

Deux jeunes filles

LOLA

Elle lave sous l'oranger
des langes de coton.
Elle a les yeux verts,
la voix violette.

Hélas! amour,
sous l'oranger en fleur!

L'eau de la rigole
était pleine de soleil,
dans l'olivier
chantait un moineau.

Hélas! amour,
sous l'oranger en fleur!

Puis, lorsque Lola
aura usé tout le savon,
viendront les toreros.

Hélas! amour,
sous l'oranger en fleur!

AMPARO

Amparo,
que tu es seule chez toi,
vêtue de blanc!
(Équateur entre le jasmin
et le nard.)

Tu entends les merveilleux
jets d'eau de ta cour,
et le faible trille jaune
du canari.

L'après-midi tu vois les cyprès
tout tremblants d'oiseaux,
et tu brodes lentement
des lettres sur ton canevas.

Amparo,
que tu es seule chez toi,
vêtue de blanc!

Et qu'il est difficile,
Amparo,
de te dire : je t'aime!

Vignettes flamencas

PORTRAIT DE SILVERIO FRANCONETTI

Italien à demi,
à demi flamenco,
comment devait chanter
ce Silverio?
Le dense miel d'Italie
avec notre citron,
coulait dans la lamentation
profonde des séguidilles.
Son cri était terrible.
Les vieillards
disent que les cheveux
se hérissaient,
que se fendait le tain
des miroirs.
Il fut un créateur
et un jardinier.
Un créateur de pavillons
pour le silence.

Maintenant sa mélodie
dort avec les échos.
Définitive et pure.
Avec l'ultime écho!

161

6

JUAN BREVA

Juan Breva avait
le corps d'un géant
et la voix d'une enfant.
Rien n'égalait son trille.
C'était la douleur
même, chantant
derrière un sourire.
Il évoque les citronniers
de Malaga la somnolente,
et sa lamentation
a le goût du sel marin.
Comme Homère, il chanta
aveugle. Sa voix avait
quelque chose de la mer sans lumière
et de l'orange exprimée.

CAFÉ-CONCERT

Lampes de cristal
et miroirs verts.
Sur l'estrade obscure,
la Parrala tient
une conversation
avec la mort.
La flamme
ne vient pas,
elle l'appelle à nouveau.
Le public
aspire les sanglots.
Et dans les miroirs verts
de longues traînes de soie
se meuvent.

LAMENTATION DE LA MORT

Sur le ciel noir,
des serpents de feu jaunes.

Je suis venu au monde avec des yeux
et je m'en vais aveugle.
Seigneur de la suprême douleur!
Et puis,
un chaleil et une couverture
par terre.

J'ai voulu arriver
où sont arrivés les bons.
Et je suis arrivé, mon Dieu!...
Mais ensuite,
un chaleil et une couverture
par terre.

Petit citron jaune
citronnier.

Jetez au vent
les petits citrons.

Vous savez bien!... C'est qu'ensuite,
ensuite,
un chaleil et une couverture
par terre.

Sur le ciel noir,
des serpents de feu jaunes.

CONJURATION

La main crispée
comme une Méduse
aveugle l'œil dolent
du chaleil.

As de trèfle.
Ciseaux en croix.

Sur la fumée blanche
de l'encens, elle a
quelque chose de la taupe et,
vaguement, du papillon.

As de trèfle.
Ciseaux en croix.

Elle étreint un cœur
invisible, la voyez-vous ?

Un cœur qui se reflète
dans le vent.

As de trèfle.
Ciseaux en croix.

MÉMENTO

Quand je mourrai,
enterrez-moi avec ma guitare
sous le sable.

Quand je mourrai,
parmi les orangers
et la bonne menthe.

Quand je mourrai,
enterrez-moi, si vous voulez,
dans une girouette.

Quand je mourrai!

Trois villes

MALAGA

La mort
entre et sort
du cabaret.

Passent de noirs chevaux
et des hommes sinistres
par les profonds chemins
de la guitare.

Et il y a une odeur de sel
et de sang de femelle
dans les nards fébriles
de cette plage.

La mort
entre et sort,
elle sort et elle entre,
la mort,
au cabaret.

QUARTIER DE CORDOUE

Topique nocturne

Dans la maison, l'on se défend
des étoiles.
La nuit s'effondre.
A l'intérieur est une enfant morte
avec une rose rouge
cachée dans sa chevelure.
Six rossignols la pleurent
sur la grille de la fenêtre.

Les gens soupirent
avec leurs guitares ouvertes.

DANSE

Carmen va dansant
par les rues de Séville.
Elle a les cheveux blancs,
brillantes les pupilles.

Fillettes,
tirez les rideaux!

Sur sa tête s'enroule
un serpent jaune,
elle rêve en dansant
aux galants d'autrefois.

Fillettes,
tirez les rideaux!

Les rues sont désertes,
et au fond l'on devine
des cœurs andalous
qui cherchent de vieilles épines.

Fillettes,
tirez les rideaux!

Six caprices

DEVINETTE DE LA GUITARE

Au carrefour
rond,
six vierges
dansent.
Trois de chair
et trois d'argent.
Les rêves d'hier les cherchent
mais ils les tiennent enlacées,
Polyphème d'or.
La guitare!

CHALEIL

Oh, qu'elle médite gravement,
la flamme du chaleil !

Comme un fakir indien
elle regarde son entraille d'or
et s'éclipse en rêvant
d'atmosphères sans vent.

Cigogne incandescente,
de son nid elle pique
les ombres massives,
et s'approche en tremblant
des yeux ronds
du petit gitan mort.

CROTALE

Crotale.
Crotale.
Crotale.
Scarabée sonore.

Dans l'araignée
de la main
tu frises l'air
chaud,
et tu t'étouffes en ton trille
de bois.

Crotale.
Crotale.
Crotale.
Scarabée sonore.

CACTUS

Laocoon sauvage.

Que tu es beau
sous la demi-lune!

Multiple pelotari.

Que tu es beau,
à menacer le vent!

Atys et Daphné
connaissent ta douleur.
Inexplicable.

AGAVE

Poulpe pétrifié.

Tu mets des ceintures cendreuses
au ventre des montagnes,

et des dents formidables
aux défilés.

Poulpe pétrifié.

CROIX

La croix.
(Point final
du chemin.)

Elle se mire dans la rigole.
(Points de suspension.)

Scène du lieutenant-colonel
de la Garde civile

SALLE DES DRAPEAUX

LIEUTENANT-COLONEL. Je suis le lieutenant-colonel de la Garde civile.

SERGENT. Oui.

LIEUTENANT-COLONEL. Personne ne me démentira.

SERGENT. Non.

LIEUTENANT-COLONEL. J'ai trois étoiles et vingt croix.

SERGENT. Oui.

LIEUTENANT-COLONEL. Le cardinal-archevêque m'a salué avec ses vingt-quatre pompons violets.

SERGENT. Oui.

LIEUTENANT-COLONEL. Je suis le colonel. Je suis le colonel. Je suis le lieutenant-colonel de la Garde civile.

Roméo et Juliette, bleu ciel, blanc et or, s'embrassent dans le jardin de tabac de la boîte à cigares. Le militaire caresse le canon d'un fusil plein d'ombre sous-marine. Une voix au-dehors.

Lune, lune, lune, lune,
du temps de l'olive.
Cazorla montre sa tour
et Benameji la cache.

179

> Lune, lune, lune, lune.
> Un coq chante dans la lune.
> Monsieur le maire, vos filles
> regardent la lune.

LIEUTENANT-COLONEL. Qu'y a-t-il ?

SERGENT. Un gitan !

Le regard de jeune mulet du gitan assombrit et dilate les petits yeux du lieutenant-colonel de la Garde civile.

LIEUTENANT-COLONEL. Je suis le lieutenant-colonel de la Garde civile.

SERGENT. Oui.

LIEUTENANT-COLONEL. Toi, qui es-tu ?

GITAN. Un gitan.

LIEUTENANT-COLONEL. Et qu'est-ce que c'est, un gitan ?

GITAN. Ce qu'on veut.

LIEUTENANT-COLONEL. Comment t'appelles-tu ?

GITAN. Comme ça.

LIEUTENANT-COLONEL. Que dis-tu ?

GITAN. Gitan.

SERGENT. Je l'ai trouvé et je l'ai amené.

LIEUTENANT-COLONEL. Où étais-tu ?

GITAN. Sur le pont des rivières.

LIEUTENANT-COLONEL. Mais de quelles rivières ?

GITAN. De toutes les rivières.

LIEUTENANT-COLONEL. Et que faisais-tu là ?

GITAN. Une tour en cannelle.

LIEUTENANT-COLONEL. Sergent !

SERGENT. A vos ordres, mon colonel de la Garde civile.

GITAN. J'ai inventé des ailes pour voler, et je vole. Soufre et rose sur mes lèvres.

LIEUTENANT-COLONEL. Ah !

GITAN.   Bien que je n'aie pas besoin d'ailes pour voler. Nuées et anneaux dans mon sang.

LIEUTENANT-COLONEL.   Aah!

GITAN.   En janvier j'ai de la fleur d'oranger.

LIEUTENANT-COLONEL, *convulsé*.   Aaaaah!

GITAN.   Et des oranges sous la neige.

LIEUTENANT-COLONEL.   Aaaaah! Poum, pim, pam.

Il tombe mort.

L'âme de tabac et de café au lait du lieutenant-colonel de la Garde civile sort par la fenêtre.

SERGENT.   Au secours!

Dans la cour de la caserne, quatre gardes civils rossent le gitan.

CHANSON DU GITAN ROSSÉ

Vingt-quatre gifles,
Vingt-quatre gifles;
et puis ma mère, ce soir,
me mettra dans du papier d'argent.

Garde civile des chemins,
donnez-moi une gorgée d'eau.
De l'eau avec des poissons et des bateaux.
De l'eau, de l'eau, de l'eau, de l'eau.

Ah! commandant des gardes civils,
qui es là-haut dans ta chambre!
N'as-tu aucun mouchoir de soie
pour m'essuyer la figure!

5 juillet 1925.

Dialogue d'Amer

UNE CAMPAGNE

UNE VOIX :

Amer.

Les lauriers-roses de ma cour.

Cœur d'amande amère.

Amer.

Arrivent trois jeunes gens avec de larges chapeaux.

PREMIER JEUNE HOMME. Nous allons être en retard.

DEUXIÈME JEUNE HOMME. La nuit tombe.

PREMIER JEUNE HOMME. Et celui-là?

DEUXIÈME JEUNE HOMME. Il nous suit.

PREMIER JEUNE HOMME, *à voix haute*. Amer!

AMER, *au loin*. J'y vais.

DEUXIÈME JEUNE HOMME, *en criant*. Amer!

AMER, *calmement*. J'y vais!

Pause.

PREMIER JEUNE HOMME. Quels beaux oliviers!

DEUXIÈME JEUNE HOMME. Oui.

Long silence.

PREMIER JEUNE HOMME. Je n'aime pas marcher la nuit.

DEUXIÈME JEUNE HOMME. Moi non plus.

PREMIER JEUNE HOMME. La nuit est faite pour dormir.

DEUXIÈME JEUNE HOMME. C'est vrai.

Grenouilles et grillons de l'été andalou.
Amer marche, les mains passées dans la
ceinture.

AMER. Aïe! Aaaaah!

J'ai questionné la mort.

Aïe! Aaaaah!

PREMIER JEUNE HOMME, *de très loin.* Amer!

DEUXIÈME JEUNE HOMME, *quasi imperceptible.* Ameeer!

Silence.

Amer est seul au milieu de la route. Il ferme
à demi ses grands yeux verts et ceint sa veste
de panne autour de sa taille. De hautes montagnes
l'environnent. Sa grosse montre d'argent résonne
obscurément dans sa poche, à chaque pas.

Un cavalier arrive en galopant sur la route.

CAVALIER, *arrêtant son cheval.* Bonsoir!

AMER. La paix de Dieu soit avec vous.

CAVALIER. Vous allez à Grenade?

AMER. Je vais à Grenade.

CAVALIER. Nous y allons donc tous deux.

AMER. Il semble.

CAVALIER. Pourquoi ne montez-vous pas en croupe?

AMER. Parce que je n'ai pas mal aux pieds.

CAVALIER. Je viens de Malaga.

AMER. Bon.

CAVALIER. Mes frères y vivent.

AMER, *sur un ton déplaisant.* Combien?

CAVALIER. Ils sont trois. Ils vendent des couteaux.
C'est leur métier.

AMER. Grand bien leur fasse.

CAVALIER. Des couteaux d'argent et d'or.

AMER.   Un couteau n'a qu'à être un couteau.

CAVALIER.   Erreur.

AMER.   Merci.

CAVALIER.   Les couteaux d'or vont au cœur tout seuls. Ceux d'argent tranchent le cou comme un brin d'herbe.

AMER.   Ils ne servent pas à couper le pain?

CAVALIER.   Les hommes rompent le pain avec leurs mains.

AMER.   C'est vrai!

> *Le cheval s'agite.*

CAVALIER.   Cheval!

AMER.   C'est la nuit.

> *Le chemin onduleux étire en spirales l'ombre de l'animal.*

CAVALIER.   Tu veux un couteau?

AMER.   Non.

CAVALIER.   Je te l'offre.

AMER.   Je ne l'accepte pas.

CAVALIER.   Tu n'auras pas d'autre occasion.

AMER.   Qui sait!

CAVALIER.   Les autres couteaux ne valent rien. Les autres couteaux sont mous et prennent peur du sang. Ceux que nous vendons sont froids. Tu comprends? Ils entrent, cherchent l'endroit le plus chaud et s'y arrêtent.

> *Amer se tait. Sa main droite devient froide comme si elle serrait un morceau d'or.*

CAVALIER.   Quel beau couteau!

AMER.   Il vaut cher?

CAVALIER.   Mais, tu ne veux pas celui-ci?

> *Il montre un couteau en or. La pointe brille comme la flamme d'un chaleil.*

AMER.   J'ai dit non.

CAVALIER.   Monte avec moi, l'ami!

AMER.   Je ne suis pas encore fatigué.

Le cheval s'épouvante.

CAVALIER, *tirant sur la bride.*   Quel cheval j'ai là!

AMER.   C'est l'obscurité.

Pause.

CAVALIER.   Comme je te le disais, à Malaga sont mes trois frères. Quelle manière de vendre des couteaux! La cathédrale en a acheté deux mille pour orner tous les autels et couronner la tour. Bien des bateaux y ont leurs noms écrits. Les pêcheurs les plus humbles s'éclairent la nuit de l'éclat de leurs lames effilées.

AMER.   C'est magnifique!

CAVALIER.   Qui peut le nier?

*La nuit s'épaissit comme un vin de cent ans.
Le gros serpent du Sud ouvre ses yeux dans le
petit matin, et les dormeurs ressentent un désir
infini de se jeter par le balcon dans la magie
perverse du lointain parfumé.*

AMER.   Il me semble que nous nous sommes égarés.

CAVALIER, *arrêtant son cheval.*   Oui?

AMER.   En parlant.

CAVALIER.   Ces lumières-là ne sont-elles pas celles de Grenade?

AMER.   Je ne sais.

CAVALIER.   Le monde est bien grand.

AMER.   Comme il est inhabité...

CAVALIER.   Tu le dis.

AMER.   Je suis pris d'un désespoir! Aïe! Aaaaah!

CAVALIER.   Parce que tu arrives là. Que fais-tu?

AMER.   Ce que je fais?

CAVALIER.   Et si tu restes à ta place, pourquoi veux-tu y rester?

AMER.   Pourquoi?

186

CAVALIER.   Moi, je monte ce cheval et je vends des couteaux, mais si je ne le faisais pas, qu'arriverait-il ?

AMER.   Ce qu'il arriverait ?

Pause.

CAVALIER.   Nous sommes devant Grenade.

AMER.   Est-il possible ?

CAVALIER.   Vois les miradors, comme ils brillent.

AMER.   Oui, certainement.

CAVALIER.   Tu ne refuseras pas maintenant de monter.

AMER.   Attends un peu.

CAVALIER.   Allons, monte! Monte vite. Il faut arriver avant l'aube... Et prends ce couteau. Je te l'offre!

AMER.   Aïe! Aaaaah!

Le Cavalier aide Amer à monter. Ils vont vers Grenade. La montagne du fond se couvre de ciguës et d'orties.

CHANSON DE LA MÈRE D'AMER

On le porte sur mon drap
mes lauriers-roses et mon palmier.

Vingt-septième jour d'août
avec un petit couteau d'or.

Signe de croix. Et marchons!
Il était brun et amer.

Voisines, donnez-moi un broc
de laiton plein de citronnade.

Signe de croix. Ne pleurez pas.
Amer est dans la lune.

9 juillet 1925.

Romancero gitan

Traduit par André Belamich — *à l'exception de* la Femme adultère, *par Jean Prévost, et du* Martyre de Sainte Eulalie, *par Jules Supervielle.*

I. ROMANCE DE LA LUNE, LUNE

A Conchita Garcia Lorca.

La lune vint à la forge
avec ses volants de nards.
L'enfant, les yeux grands ouverts,
la regarde la regarde.
Dans la brise qui s'émeut
la lune bouge les bras,
dévoilant, lascive et pure,
ses seins blancs de dur métal.
Va-t'en lune, lune, lune.
Si les gitans arrivaient,
ils feraient avec ton cœur
bagues blanches et colliers.
Enfant, laisse-moi danser.
Quand viendront les cavaliers,
ils te verront sur l'enclume
étendu, les yeux fermés.
Va-t'en lune, lune, lune.
Je les entends chevaucher.
Enfant, laisse-moi, tu froisses
ma blancheur amidonnée.

Battant le tambour des plaines
approchait le cavalier.
Dans la forge silencieuse
gît l'enfant, les yeux fermés.

Par l'olivette venaient,
bronze et rêve, les gitans,
chevauchant la tête haute
et le regard somnolent.

Comme chante sur son arbre,
comme chante la chouette!
Dans le ciel marche la lune
tenant l'enfant par la main.

Autour de l'enclume pleurent
les gitans désespérés.
La brise qui veille, veille,
la brise fait la veillée.

II. PRÉCIEUSE ET LE VENT

A Dámaso Alonso.

De sa lune en parchemin,
par un hybride sentier
de lauriers et de cristal,
Précieuse s'en vient jouer.
Le silence sans étoiles,
pour fuir ce tintement tombe
où la mer se brise et chante
sa nuit pleine de poissons.
Sur les pics de la montagne
dorment les carabiniers
qui gardent les blanches tours
où demeurent les Anglais.
Et les gitans du rivage
élèvent pour se distraire
des berceaux de coquillages
et des branches de pin vert.

*

De sa lune en parchemin
Précieuse s'en vient jouer.

A sa vue le vent se lève,
car jamais il ne sommeille.
Gros saint Christophe tout nu
et plein de célestes langues,
il la regarde en jouant
d'une douce flûte absente.

Dis, laisse-moi relever
ta robe pour voir ton corps.
Ouvre entre mes doigts anciens
la rose bleue de ton ventre.

Lâchant son tambour, Précieuse
prend la fuite à toutes jambes.
Le vent mâle la poursuit
avec une épée brûlante.

La mer fronce sa rumeur.
Pâlissent les oliviers.
Les flûtes de l'ombre chantent,
et le gong lisse des neiges.

Précieuse, cours vite, vite,
le vent vert va t'attraper!
Précieuse, cours vite, vite,
regarde-le arriver,
satyre d'étoiles basses
aux mille langues lustrées!

*

Précieuse, morte de peur,
est allée se réfugier,

au-dessus de la pinède,
chez le consul des Anglais.

Alarmés par ces appels,
viennent trois carabiniers
serrés dans leur cape noire,
le calot bien enfoncé.

L'Anglais donne à la gitane
une tasse de lait tiède
avec un verre de gin
qu'elle laisse de côté.

Et tandis qu'elle raconte
son aventure en pleurant,
le vent sur le toit d'ardoises
plante, furieux, les dents.

III. LA RIXE

A Rafael Méndez.

Dans le milieu du ravin,
superbes de sang adverse,
luisent comme des poissons
les navajas d'Albalcète.
Un jour cru de jeu de cartes
découpe sur l'aigre vert
des profils de cavaliers
dont les bêtes s'exaspèrent.
Au faîte d'un olivier
deux vieilles femmes se plaignent.
Le taureau de la querelle
se dresse sur les murettes.
Et des anges noirs apportent
des mouchoirs, de l'eau de neige,
des anges aux longues ailes
de navajas d'Albacète.
Juan Antonio de Montilla
dévale en mourant la pente
— le corps étoilé d'iris,
une grenade à la tempe —
et sur une croix de flamme
prend la route de la mort.

*

Le juge par l'olivette
arrive avec ses sergents.
Le sang répandu gémit
son chant muet de serpent.
Ici, messieurs les gendarmes,
c'est toujours pareil, voyez :
Il y a cinq Carthaginois
et quatre Romains tués.

*

Le soir ivre de figuiers
et de rumeurs surchauffées
tombe pâmé sur les cuisses
sanglantes des cavaliers,
tandis que des anges noirs,
des anges aux longues tresses,
planent dans l'air du couchant
avec leur cœur d'huile claire.

IV. ROMANCE SOMNAMBULE

A Gloria Giner
et Fernando de los Rios.

Vert c'est toi que j'aime vert,
vert du vent et vert des branches,
le cheval dans la montagne
et la barque sur la mer.
L'ombre à la taille, elle rêve,
penchée à sa balustrade,
vert visage, cheveux verts,
prunelles de froid métal,
vert c'est toi que j'aime vert,
et sous la lune gitane
tous les objets la regardent,
elle qui ne peut les voir.

*

Vert c'est toi que j'aime vert.
Un essaim d'astres de givre
escorte le poisson d'ombre
qui ouvre la voie de l'aube.

Le figuier griffe le vent
avec sa râpe de branches.
Le mont, comme un chat sauvage,
hérisse tous ses agaves.
Mais qui viendra? Et par où?
Penchée à sa balustrade,
vert visage, cheveux verts,
la mer est son rêve amer.

*

Ami, veux-tu me donner
ta maison pour mon cheval,
ton miroir pour mon harnais,
ton manteau pour mon poignard?
Je reviens ensanglanté
depuis les cols de Cabra.
Mon garçon, si je pouvais,
j'accepterais ton marché.
Mais je ne suis plus moi-même,
ma maison n'est plus la mienne.
Ami, je voudrais mourir
dans un lit, tranquillement,
sur un bon sommier d'acier,
entre des draps de Hollande.
Vois-tu cette plaie qui s'ouvre
de ma poitrine à ma gorge?
Je vois trois cents roses brunes
fleurir ta chemise blanche.
La laine de ta ceinture
a pris l'odeur de ton sang.
Mais je ne suis plus moi-même,
ma maison n'est plus la mienne.

Laissez-moi monter au moins
vers ces hautes balustrades,
laissez, laissez-moi monter
à ces vertes balustrades,
aux balustres de la lune
d'où l'eau retombe en cascade.

*

Les deux compagnons s'élèvent
vers les hautes balustrades.
Laissant des traces de sang.
Laissant des traces de larmes.
Quelques lanternes d'étain
tremblotaient sur les terrasses.
Mille tambourins de verre
blessaient le petit matin.

*

Vert c'est toi que j'aime vert,
vert du vent et vert des branches.
Les deux compagnons montaient.
Dans leur bouche le grand vent
laissait comme un goût de fiel,
de basilic et de menthe.
Ami, dis-moi, où est-elle,
ta fille, ta fille amère?
Que de fois elle attendit!
Que de fois elle espéra,
frais visage, cheveux noirs,
à la verte balustrade!

Au miroir de la citerne
se balançait la gitane,
vert visage, cheveux verts,
prunelles de froid métal.
Un mince glaçon de lune
la soutient à la surface.
La nuit se fit plus intime
comme une petite place.
Ivres, des gardes civils
cognaient aux portes, là-bas...
Vert c'est toi que j'aime vert,
vert du vent et vert des branches,
le cheval dans la montagne
et la barque sur la mer.

V. LA NONNE GITANE

A José Moreno Villa.

Calme de myrte et de chaux.
Mauves dans les herbes fines.
Elle brode des violiers
sur sa toile jaune vif.
Dans le lustre gris voltigent
les sept colibris du prisme.
L'église grogne là-bas
comme un ours ventre au midi.
Quel fin travail! Quelle grâce!
Mais sur la claire batiste
la nonne aimerait broder
des fleurs de sa fantaisie.
Quels soleils! Quels magnolias
de rubans, de pierreries!
Quels safrans et quelles lunes
sur la nappe de l'Office!
Dans la cuisine prochaine
cinq oranges se confisent.
Les cinq blessures du Christ
ouvertes en Almérie.

Dans les yeux de la brodeuse
vont deux cavaliers agiles.
Une ultime rumeur sourde
lui décolle la chemise.
A la vue des monts lointains
sous les nuées immobiles,
il lui semble que son cœur,
sucre et verveine, se brise.
Oh, quelle plaines debout
sous vingt soleils qui scintillent,
quelles rivières cabrées
entrevoit sa fantaisie!
Mais elle brode toujours,
tandis que, droit dans la brise,
le soleil joue aux échecs
sur la haute jalousie.

VI. LA FEMME ADULTÈRE

A Lydia Cabrera
et à sa petite négresse.

Je la pris près de la rivière,
Car je la croyais sans mari
Tandis qu'elle était adultère.
Ce fut la Saint-Jacques, la nuit,
Par rendez-vous et compromis,
Quand s'éteignirent les lumières
Et s'allumèrent les cricris.
Au coin des dernières enceintes,
Je touchai ses seins endormis ;
Sa poitrine pour moi s'ouvrit
Comme des branches de jacinthes.
Et dans mes oreilles l'empois
De ses jupes amidonnées
Crissait comme soie arrachée
Par douze couteaux à la fois.
Les cimes d'arbres sans lumière
Grandissaient au bord des chemins
Et tout un horizon de chiens
Aboyait loin de la rivière.

Quand nous avons franchi les ronces
Les épines et les ajoncs,
Sous elle son chignon s'enfonce
Et fait un trou dans le limon.
Quand ma cravate fut ôtée,
Elle retira ses jupons,
Puis (quand j'ôtai mon ceinturon)
Quatre corsages d'affilée.
Ni le nard ni les escargots
N'eurent jamais la peau si fine,
Ni, sous la lune, les cristaux
N'ont de lueurs si cristallines.
Ses cuisses s'enfuyaient sous moi
Comme des truites effrayées
Une moitié tout embrasée,
L'autre moitié pleine de froid.
Cette nuit me vit galoper
De ma plus belle chevauchée,
Sur une pouliche nacrée,
Sans brides et sans étriers.
Je suis homme et ne peux redire
Les choses qu'elle me disait :
Le clair entendement m'inspire
De me montrer fort circonspect.
Sale de baisers et de sable,
Du bord de l'eau je la sortis;
Les iris balançaient leurs sabres
Contre les brises de la nuit.

Pour agir en pleine droiture
Comme fait un loyal gitan,
Je lui fis don, en la quittant,
D'un grand beau panier à couture,

Mais sans vouloir en être épris :
Parce qu'elle était adultère
Et se prétendait sans mari
Quand nous allions vers la rivière.

VII. ROMANCE DE LA PEINE NOIRE

A José Navarro Pardo.

Les pics sonores des coqs
font une brèche à l'aurore,
quand de la colline sombre
descend Soledad Montoya.
Cuivre jaune, tout son corps
fleure la cavale et l'ombre.
Ses seins, enclumes noircies,
gémissent des chansons rondes.
Soledad, qui cherches-tu,
solitaire, au point du jour?
Que je cherche qui je cherche,
dis-moi si cela t'importe!
Je cours après un seul but,
mon bonheur et ma raison.
Soledad de mes chagrins,
la cavale qui s'emporte
finit par trouver la mer
et les vagues la dévorent.
Ne parle pas de la mer,
car la peine noire pousse

dans la terre aux oliviers
sous la rumeur de leurs branches.
Soledad, quelle pitié!
Quelle peine désolante!
Tu as des pleurs de citron,
aigres de lèvre et d'attente.
Quelle peine! Je traverse
ma maison comme une folle,
mes cheveux traînant par terre
de la cuisine à l'alcôve.
Une peine qui rend comme
du jais ma chair et ma robe.
Ah, mes chemises de fil!
Ah, mes cuisses de pavot!
Dans la source aux alouettes,
Soledad, lave ton corps,
et puis laisse reposer
ton cœur, Soledad Montoya.

★

Tout en bas chante un ruisseau,
volant de ciel et de feuilles.
Des fleurs de la calebasse
se couronne le jour neuf.
O la peine des gitans!
Peine pure et solitaire.
Peine de rive secrète
et de matinée lointaine!

VIII. SAINT MICHEL

(Grenade)

A Diego Buigas de Dalmáu.

On voit depuis les balcons,
par le mont qui monte, monte,
des mulets avec des ombres
et leur faix de tournesols.
Leur yeux dans la pente sombre
se voilent d'immense nuit.
Aux encoignures de l'air
crisse l'aurore saline.

Un grand ciel de mulets blancs
ferme leurs yeux de mercure,
couronnant d'un jeu de cœurs
le tranquille clair-obscur.
Et l'onde se fait glacée
afin que nul ne la frôle.
Onde folle et découverte
par le mont qui monte, monte.

Dans la loge de sa tour,
Saint Michel plein de dentelles
laisse voir ses belles cuisses
moulées par les lampadaires.
Archange dressé au geste
d'annoncer les douze coups,
il simule une ire douce
de plume et de rossignol.
Éphèbe aux trois mille nuits,
Saint Michel chante aux vitraux,
parfumé d'eau de Cologne,
bien au-dessus des corolles.

*

La mer sur la plage danse
un poème de balcons.
Les rives lunaires gagnent
des rumeurs, perdent des joncs.
Il vient des filles qui mangent
des graines de tournesol.
Leurs larges croupes secrètes
sont des planètes de bronze.
Il vient de hauts cavaliers,
des dames au triste port,
brunies par la nostalgie
d'un hier de rossignols.
Et l'évêque de Manille,
aveugle en safran et pauvre,
dit une messe à deux filles
pour les femmes et les hommes.

★

Dans la loge de sa tour,
Saint Michel est silencieux
parmi ses jupons raidis
de miroirs et d'entre-deux.

Saint Michel, prince des globes
et roi des chiffres impairs,
dans une fine arabesque
de cris et de belvédères.

IX. SAINT RAPHAEL

(Cordoue)

A Juan Izquierdo Croselles.

I

Des chars fermés arrivaient
jusqu'aux joncs de la rivière
où l'onde lisse et polit
un torse nu de Romain.
Chars que le Guadalquivir
couche sur son cristal mûr,
entre l'émail de ses fleurs
et les échos de la nue.
Les enfants tissent et chantent
la désillusion du monde,
autour des vieilles voitures
délaissées dans le nocturne.
Mais Cordoue ne tremble pas
sous le mystère confus :
si l'ombre avec la fumée
suscite une architecture,
un pied de marbre s'affirme
dans son éclat chaste et dur.
De fins pétales d'étain

en gris lumineux festonnent
la brise qui se déploie
au front des arcs de triomphe.
Et tandis que le pont souffle
ses dix rumeurs de Neptune,
les vendeurs de cigarettes
fuient par les brèches du mur.

II

Un seul poisson dans le flot
qui unit les deux égales :
Cordoue aux douceurs de jonc,
Cordoue au profil de marbre.
Impassibles, des enfants
au bord de l'eau se dénudent,
apprentis du vieux Tobie
et Merlins par la ceinture.
Ils agacent le poisson
par des questions saugrenues :
voudrait-il des fleurs de vin
ou des sauts de demi-lune ?
Mais le poisson qui endeuille
le marbre et dore les ondes
leur enseigne l'équilibre
solitaire des colonnes.
L'Archange à demi arabe
sous ses paillettes obscures,
dans le rendez-vous des eaux
cherchait rumeur et refuge.

Un seul poisson dans le flot.
Deux Cordoue de beauté pure.
Cordoue en jets d'eau brisée.
Sèche Cordoue dans l'azur.

X. SAINT GABRIEL

(Séville)

A D. Agustin Viñuales.

I

Un bel enfant de jonc souple,
large épaule, taille mince,
le teint de pomme nocturne,
grands yeux, bouche douce-amère,
et les nerfs d'argent brûlant,
passe dans la rue déserte.
Ses souliers de cuir verni
brisent les dahlias de l'air
au rythme double qui chante
de brèves douleurs célestes.
Sur les rives de la mer
il n'est palme qui l'égale,
ni empereur couronné,
ni astre brillant en marche.
Lorsqu'il incline la tête
sur sa poitrine de jaspe,
la nuit pour s'agenouiller
devant lui cherche des plaines.

Les guitares sonnent seules
pour l'Archange Gabriel,
ennemi juré des saules
et dompteur de tourterelles.
Saint Gabriel, l'enfant pleure
dans le ventre de sa mère.
N'oublie pas que ton costume
les gitans te l'ont offert.

II

Annonciation des Rois Mages,
riche lune et pauvre mise,
ouvre la porte à l'étoile
qui par la ruelle arrive.
L'Archange Saint Gabriel,
à la fois sourire et lys,
petit-fils de la Giralda,
s'en vient lui rendre visite.
A son gilet festonné
des grillons cachés palpitent.
En clochettes se changèrent
les étoiles de la nuit.
Saint Gabriel, me voici
percée de trois clous de joie.
Tu fais briller des jasmins
sur mon visage ébloui.
Dieu te garde, Annonciation,
créature de prodige.
Tu auras un fils plus beau
que les tiges de la brise,
Gabriel de mes prunelles,

Gabrielillo de ma vie,
pour t'asseoir je rêverais
d'un fauteuil d'œillets fleuris.
Dieu te garde, Annonciation,
riche lune et pauvre mise.
Ton fils aura une tache
et trois plaies à la poitrine.
Gabriel, comme tu brilles!
Gabrielillo de ma vie!
Au fond de mes seins je sens
le lait tiède qui jaillit.
Dieu te garde, Annonciation,
mère de cent dynasties.
Un paysage de chevauchée
s'éclaire en tes yeux arides.

*

L'enfant chante dans le sein
d'Annonciation étonnée.
Trois balles d'amande verte
tremblent dans sa voix fluette.

Et Saint Gabriel dans l'air
s'élève par une échelle.
Les étoiles de la nuit
se changent en immortelles.

XI. PRISE D'ANTONITO EL CAMBORIO SUR LA ROUTE DE SÉVILLE

A Margarita Xirgu.

Antonio Torres Heredia,
fils et neveu des Camborios,
badine d'osier en main,
va vers Séville, aux taureaux.
Le teint brun de verte lune,
il avance, grave et beau.
Ses cheveux lustrés en boucles
reluisent entre ses yeux.
A mi-chemin il s'arrête
pour couper les citrons clairs
qu'il lance à foison dans l'eau,
à la rendre toute d'or.
Et c'est à la mi-chemin,
sous le feuillage d'un orme,
que les gendarmes des routes
l'entraînent vers la prison.

*

Le jour s'en va lentement,
le soir pendu à l'épaule,

faisant une longue passe
à la mer et aux ruisseaux.
Les oliviers se préparent
à la nuit du Capricorne.
Une courte brise, équestre,
saute les cimes de plomb.
Antonio Torres Heredia,
fils et neveu des Camborios,
sans sa badine d'osier,
marche entre les cinq tricornes.

Antonio, qui donc es-tu?
Si tu t'appelais Camborio,
tu aurais fait une source
de sang, avec cinq ruisseaux.
Tu n'es le fils de personne,
ni véritable Camborio.
Ils sont éteints, les gitans
qui allaient seuls par les monts!
Sous leur couche de poussière
frémissent les vieux couteaux.

Neuf heures du soir sonnaient.
On l'emmena au cachot,
tandis que les policiers
buvaient du citron à l'eau.
Et à neuf heures du soir
on verrouilla le cachot.
Tel la croupe d'un poulain
le soir reluisait encore.

XII. MORT D'ANTONITO EL CAMBORIO

A José Antonio Rubio Sacristan.

Des voix de mort s'élevèrent
aux bords du Guadalquivir.
Des voix anciennes qui cernent
une voix d'œillet viril.
Il plantait à leurs bottines
de vrais crocs de sanglier.
Dans la mêlée il faisait
des sauts de dauphin huilés.
Il baigna de sang adverse
sa cravate cramoisie,
mais, devant quatre poignards,
à la fin il dut fléchir.
Comme les astres plongeaient
leur pique dans l'onde grise
et que les taureaux rêvaient
de « véroniques » fleuries,
des voix de mort s'élevèrent
aux bords du Guadalquivir.

Antonio Torres Heredia,
Camborio de toison riche,
au teint brun de verte lune,
à la voix d'œillet viril,
qui t'a enlevé la vie
aux bords du Guadalquivir?
Mes quatre cousins Heredia,
les fils de Benameji.
Ce qu'ils n'enviaient aux autres
chez moi leur faisait envie.
Mes souliers rouge cerise,
mes camées d'ivoire fin
et jusqu'à mon teint pétri
à l'olive et au jasmin.
O Antoñito el Camborio,
digne d'une Impératrice!
Rappelle-toi à la Vierge,
car tu vas bientôt mourir.
O Federico Garcia,
préviens la Garde Civile!
Ma taille s'est brisée comme
une canne de maïs.

Saisi de trois coups de sang,
il succombe de profil.
Vive monnaie qui jamais
ne sera plus reproduite.
Un ange glorieux pose
sa tête sur un coussin.
D'autres aux rougeurs fanées
lui ont allumé un cierge.

Et quand les quatre cousins
eurent joint Benameji,
les voix de mort s'effacèrent
aux bords du Guadalquivir.

XIII. MORT D'AMOUR

A Margarita Manso.

Qu'est-ce qui brille là-bas
dans les profonds corridors ?
Ferme la porte, mon fils,
entends-tu ? Onze heures sonnent.
Dans mes yeux, sans le vouloir,
je vois luire quatre lampes.
Sans doute, chez les voisins
c'est du cuivre que l'on frotte.

*

Ail d'argent qui agonise,
la lune en décroissant pose
à la tête des tours jaunes
de longues crinières fauves.
La nuit vient frapper tremblante
à la vitre des balcons,
poursuivie par la meute
des mille chiens qui l'ignorent.
Une odeur de vin et d'ambre
s'exhale des corridors.

La rumeur des voix anciennes,
le souffle humide des joncs,
retentissent sous l'arcade
brisée de minuit profond.
Les bœufs dormaient et les roses.
Seules dans les corridors
les quatre lueurs clamaient
une fureur de Saint Georges.
Les tristes femmes du val
descendaient le sang de l'homme,
calme de la fleur coupée,
douleur de la cuisse jeune.
Les vieilles de la rivière
pleurèrent au pied des monts
un instant infranchissable
de chevelure et de noms.
Façades de chaux, la nuit
se taillait en carrés blancs.
Séraphins et bohémiens
jouaient de l'accordéon.
Mère, lorsque je mourrai,
fais-le savoir aux patrons
par des télégrammes bleus
qui volent du Sud au Nord.
Sept cris et sept jets de sang
avec sept doubles pavots
brisèrent d'opaques glaces
au plus obscur des salons.
Couverte de mains coupées
flottant parmi des couronnes,
résonnait je ne sais où
la mer sombre des serments.

Aux brusques rumeurs du bois
le vent secouait les portes,
tandis que clamaient les lueurs
dans les profonds corridors.

XIV. ROMANCE DE L'ASSIGNÉ

Pour Emilio Aladrén.

Solitude sans relâche!
Des yeux — les miens plus petits,
plus grands ceux de mon cheval —
ne se ferment de la nuit
sans regarder du côté
où s'évanouit tranquille
un rêve de treize barques.
Mais toujours durs et limpides,
écuyers montant la garde,
mes yeux regardent un nord
de rochers et de métal
où mon corps privé de veines
consulte de froides cartes.

*

Les denses bœufs de rivière
chargent les garçons légers
qui se baignent sur la lune
de leurs cornes ondulées,

tandis que les marteaux chantent
dans les forges somnambules
l'insomnie du cavalier
et celle de sa monture.

★

Le vingt-cinq du mois de Juin,
on vint prévenir Amargo :
Tu peux couper, si tu veux,
les lauriers-blancs de ta cour.
Peins une croix sur ta porte
et mets au-dessous ton nom,
car la ciguë et l'ortie
naîtront bientôt de tes flancs
et des pointes de chaux vive
déchireront tes souliers.
Ce sera dans la nuit noire,
parmi les monts aimantés
où les bœufs de la rivière
boivent des joncs dans leur rêve.
Commande lampes et cloches.
Apprends à croiser les mains
et à goûter les vents froids
des métaux et des rochers.
Car tu seras dans deux mois
raide mort et enterré.

★

Une épée de nébuleuse
s'élève au poing de Saint Jacques
et des flancs du ciel cambré
ruisselle un silence grave.

Le vingt-cinq du mois de Juin
il avait les yeux ouverts
et le vingt-cinq du mois d'Août
il gisait pour les fermer.
Les gens descendaient la rue
pour aller voir l'assigné
qui contemplait sur le mur
sa solitude apaisée.
Et le suaire, sans défaut,
sculpté d'un ciseau romain,
tenait la mort immobile
dans sa draperie sévère.

XV. ROMANCE DE LA GARDE CIVILE ESPAGNOLE

A Juan Guerrero,
Consul général de la Poésie.

Ils montent de noirs chevaux
dont les ferrures sont noires.
Des taches d'encre et de cire
luisent le long de leurs capes.
S'ils ne pleurent, c'est qu'ils ont
du plomb au lieu de cervelle
et une âme en cuir vernis.
Par la chaussée ils s'en viennent.
Groupe bossu et nocturne,
sur leur passage ils font naître
d'obscurs silences de gomme
et des peurs de sable fin.
Ils vont par où bon leur semble,
cachant au creux de leur tête
une vague astronomie
de pistolets irréels.

O la ville de gitans!
Aux coins de rues, des bannières.
La lune et la calebasse
et la cerise en conserve.
O la ville des gitans,
qui jamais peut t'oublier?
Ville de douleur musquée
avec tes tours de cannelle.

*

Comme descendait la nuit,
la nuit la nuit tout entière,
les gitans à leurs enclumes
forgeaient flèches et soleils.
Un cheval ensanglanté
frappait aux portes muettes.
Des coqs de verre chantaient
à Jerez de la Frontière.
A l'angle de la surprise
le vent nu tourne soudain
dans la nuit d'argent de nuit,
la nuit la nuit tout entière.

*

La Vierge et Saint Joseph
ont perdu leurs castagnettes.
Ils vont prier les gitans
de se mettre à leur recherche.
La Vierge avance habillée
d'un costume d'alcaldesse

en papier de chocolat
et colliers d'amandes vertes.
Saint Joseph remue les bras
sous sa cape de satin.
Vient après Pedro Domecq
avec trois sultans de Perse.
La demi-lune songeait
dans une extase d'aigrette.
Les terrasses s'emplissaient
d'étendards et de lanternes.
Et des danseuses sans hanches
à leurs miroirs sanglotaient.
L'eau et l'ombre, l'ombre et l'eau
à Jerez de la Frontière.

*

O la ville des gitans!
Aux coins de rues, des bannières.
Voici la Garde Civile.
Éteins tes vertes lumières.
O la ville des gitans!
Qui jamais peut t'oublier?
Laissez-la loin de la mer
avec ses cheveux sans peigne.

*

Ils avancent deux par deux
vers la ville de la fête.
Une rumeur d'immortelles
envahit les cartouchières.
Ils avancent deux par deux.
Double nocturne de fond.

Le ciel pour leur fantaisie
n'est qu'un bazar d'éperons.

*

La ville multipliait
ses portes, libre de crainte.
Quarante gardes civils
pour la piller y pénètrent.
Les horloges s'arrêtèrent
et le cognac des bouteilles
se camoufla en novembre
pour que nul ne le suspecte.
Une volée de longs cris
s'éleva des girouettes.
Les sabres fendent les brises
que les lourds sabots renversent.
Par des chemins de pénombre
s'enfuient les gitanes vieilles
avec leurs chevaux dormants
et leurs jarres de piécettes.
Au haut des rues escarpées
grimpent les capes funèbres,
faisant reluire fugaces
des moulinets derrière elles.

Les gitans se réfugient
au portail de Bethléem.
Saint Joseph, couvert de plaies,
enterre une jouvencelle.
Des fusils perçants résonnent,
toute la nuit, obstinés.
La Vierge applique aux enfants

de la salive d'étoiles.
Pourtant la Garde Civile
avance en semant des flammes
dans lesquelles, jeune et nue,
l'imagination s'embrase.
Rosa, fille des Camborios,
gémit, assise à sa porte,
devant ses deux seins coupés
et posés sur un plateau.
Et d'autres filles couraient,
poursuivies par leurs tresses,
dans un air où éclataient
des roses de poudre noire.
Lorsque toutes les terrasses
furent des sillons en terre,
l'aube ondula les épaules
en un long profil de pierre.

*

O la ville des gitans!
Les gardes civils se perdent
dans un tunnel de silence
tandis que les feux t'encerclent.

O la ville des gitans!
Comment perdre ta mémoire?
Qu'on te cherche dans mon front.
Jeu de lune, jeu de sable.

Trois romances historiques

XVI. LE MARTYRE
DE SAINTE EULALIE

A Rafael Martinez Nadal.

PANORAMA DE MÉRIDA

Dans la rue court et bondit
Un cheval à la queue longue
Tandis que jouent ou sommeillent
Quelques vieux soldats de Rome.
Une futaie de Minerves
Ouvre mille bras sans feuilles.
De l'eau suspendue redore
Les arêtes de rochers.
Une nuit faite de torses,
D'étoiles au nez cassé,
Attend les fentes de l'aube
Pour s'écrouler tout entière.
De temps à autre résonnent
Des jurons à crête rouge.
Les soupirs de l'enfant sainte
Brisent le cristal des coupes.
La roue aiguise ses lames
Et ses crochets suraigus.

Le taureau des forges brame
Et Mérida se couronne
De nards presque réveillés
Et de mûres sur leurs tiges.

LE MARTYRE

Voici Flore nue qui monte
De petits escaliers d'eau.
Le Consul veut un plateau
Pour les deux seins d'Eulalie.
De la gorge de la sainte
Sort un jet de veines vertes.
Son sexe tremble, embrouillé
Comme un oiseau dans les ronces.
Sur le sol, déjà sans norme,
Sautent ses deux mains coupées
Pouvant encore se croiser
Dans une prière ténue,
Ténue mais décapitée.
Et par les trous purpurins
Où naguère étaient ses seins
On voit des ciels tout petits
et des ruisseaux de lait blanc.
Mille petits arbres de sang
Opposent leurs troncs humides
Aux mille bistouris du feu.
De jaunes centurions,
Chair grise ayant mal dormi,
Vont au ciel entrechoquant
Leurs armures en argent.
Pendant que vibre confuse
Une passion de crinières

Et d'épées longues et courtes
Le Consul sur son plateau
Tient les seins fumés d'Eulalie.

ENFER ET GLOIRE

La neige ondulée repose.
Eulalie pend à son arbre.
Sa nudité de charbon
Charbonne les airs glacés.
La nuit tendre brille haut.
Eulalie morte dans l'arbre.
Tous les encriers des villes
Versent l'encre doucement.
Noirs mannequins de tailleurs
Vous couvrez la neige au loin.
Vos longues files gémissent
Un silence mutilé.
La neige vient à tomber.
Eulalie blanche dans l'arbre.
Des escadrons de nickel
Joignent à son flanc leurs lances.

On voit luire un ostensoir
Sur un fond de ciels brûlés
Entre des gorges d'eau douce,
Des bouquets de rossignols.
Sautez, vitres de couleurs!
Eulalie blanche sur neiges.
Des anges, des séraphins
Disent : Saintes, sainte, sainte.

XVII. DON PIERRE A CHEVAL

Romance burlesque avec étangs

A Jean Cassou.

Le long d'un sentier
avançait Don Pierre.
Ah, comme il pleurait,
ce chevalier!
Monté sur un souple
cheval sans gourmette,
il quêtait le pain
avec les baisers.
Toutes les fenêtres
au vent demandaient :
De quoi se plaint-il,
ce chevalier?

PREMIER ÉTANG

Dessous l'eau
restent les paroles.
Et sur l'eau
une lune ronde
se baigne,

qui fait envie à l'autre,
si haute!
Un enfant
sur le rivage
voit la lune double et dit :
La nuit, joue-moi des cymbales!

SUITE

Dans une cité lointaine
est arrivé Don Pierre.
Une cité toute en or
entre des bois de cèdre.
Bethléem? Dans la brise,
la menthe et le romarin.
Les terrasses reluisent
et les nuages. Sous des arcs
brisés passe Don Pierre.
Un vieillard et deux commères
portant lampes d'argent
sortent à sa rencontre.
Les peupliers disent : Non.
Le rossignol : Nous verrons.

DEUXIÈME ÉTANG

Dessous l'eau
restent les paroles.
Sous la coiffure de l'eau,
un cercle d'oiseaux et de flammes.
Et parmi les roseaux,
des témoins qui savent l'absence.

Songe figé sans boussole
dans le bois d'une guitare.

Par le sentier égal
un vieillard et deux commères
portant lampes d'argent
s'en vont au cimetière.
Au milieu des safrans
ils trouvent mort, en chemin,
le sombre cheval
de Don Pierre.
La voix du soir secrète
bêle parmi le ciel.
La licorne d'absence
brise sa corne de verre.
La grande cité lointaine
est en flammes.
Un homme en pleurs s'enfonce
vers l'intérieur des terres.
Au Nord est une étoile.
Au Sud est un marin.

Dessous l'eau
gisent les paroles.
Limon de voix perdues.
Sur la fleur devenue fraîche,
Don Pierre oublié joue,
hélas, avec les rainettes!

XVIII. THAMAR ET AMNON

Pour Alfonso Garcia-Valdecasas.

La lune qui tourne au ciel
luit sur les terres de soif,
cependant que l'été sème
rumeurs de tigres et flammes.
Vibrant au-dessus des toits,
des nerfs de métal résonnent.
La brise ondulée apporte
les bêlements de la laine.
La terre s'étend couverte
d'entailles cicatrisées
et frémit sous le cautère
aigu des blanches lumières.

*

Thamar s'attarde à rêver
d'oiseaux chantant dans son sein,
au son des tambourins froids
et des cithares lunaires.
Sa nudité sur le toit

— pôle aigu de palme — appelle
de blancs flocons à son ventre
et sur son dos de la grêle.
Thamar s'attarde à chanter
toute nue sur la terrasse.
Autour de ses pieds volettent
cinq tourterelles de glace.
Amnon, vigoureux et mince,
depuis sa tour la regarde,
l'aine remplie d'écume
et d'oscillations la barbe.
Nu sous la blanche clarté,
il se tend sur la terrasse,
exhalant entre les dents
le son d'un dard qui se plante.
Et comme Amnon regardait
le rond de la lune basse,
dans la lune il vit les seins
fermes de sa sœur Thamar.

*

A trois heures et demie
il rentra pour s'allonger.
Toute l'alcôve souffrait
de ses yeux envahis d'ailes.
Le jour submerge massif
les bourgs sous le brun des sables
ou bien découvre — éphémère
corail — roses et dahlias.
L'onde des puits prisonnière
renaît silence en les jarres.
Parmi la mousse des troncs

chante couché le cobra.
Amnon gémit sous la toile
de son lit aux fraîcheurs d'ombre.
Le lierre du frisson
recouvre sa chair ardente.
Thamar pénètre en silence
dans la chambre qui se tait,
couleur veinée de Danube
trouble de traces lointaines.
Thamar, efface mes yeux
sous ton aube qui me hante.
Je vois mon sang qui dessine
sur ta jupe des volants.
Frère, laisse-moi tranquille.
Je sens courir sur ma nuque
tes baisers, guêpes et brises,
en un double essaim de flûtes.
Thamar, il y a dans tes seins
deux poissons qui m'ensorcellent.
Au bout de tes doigts j'entends
bruire une rose secrète.

*

Les cent cavales du roi
rangées dans la cour hennissent.
Sous la maigre treille flambe
le soleil dans les bassines.
Il la prend par les cheveux,
lui déchire la chemise.
De tièdes coraux dessinent
les ruisseaux d'un blond pays.

Oh, quels cris ont retenti
au-dessus des cheminées!
Quelle épaisseur de poignards,
de tuniques lacérées!
Des esclaves vont et viennent,
tristes dans les escaliers.
Des cuisses et des pistons
jouent sous les nuées arrêtées.
En cercle autour de Thamar
crient des vierges bohémiennes.
D'autres recueillent les gouttes
de sa fleur martyrisée.
Dans les alcôves fermées
s'empourprent les tissus blancs.
Aux rumeurs de tiède aurore
poissons et pampres se changent.

★

Violateur exaspéré,
Amnon s'enfuit à cheval.
Des noirs lui lancent des flèches
depuis les tours des murailles.
Et quand les quatre sabots
s'effacèrent dans l'espace,
David avec des ciseaux
trancha les fils de sa harpe.

Préface   7

CHANSONS

(1921-1924)

THÉORIES

Chanson des sept demoiselles   15
Nocturne schématique   16
La chanson du collégien   17
Le caillou veut être lumière   18
Le manège   19
Balance   21
Chanson avec mouvement   22
Proverbe   24
Frise   25
Chasseur   26
Fable   27
Août   28
Arlequin   29
Trois arbres abattus   30
Nocturnes de la fenêtre   31

                                                 245

CHANSONS POUR ENFANTS

Chanson chinoise en Europe   35
Chansonnette sévillane   37
Coquillage   38
Le lézard est tout en larmes...   39
Chanson chantée   41
Paysage   42
Chanson bête   43

ANDALUZAS

Chanson de cavalier (1860)   45
Adeline qui se promène   47
Ronce au tronc gris   48
Allant au bord de la mer...   49
Soir   50
Chanson de cavalier   51
C'est bien vrai   52
Arbrisseau   53
Joli cœur   55

TROIS PORTRAITS AVEC OMBRE

I. Verlaine   56
Bacchus   57
II. Juan Ramon Jimenez   58
Vénus   59
III. Debussy   60
Narcisse   61

JEUX

Riveraines   63
A Irène Garcia   65
A l'oreille d'une jeune fille   66
Les gens s'en allaient...   67
Chanson du mariquita   68
Arbre de chant   69
Orange et citron   70
La rue des muets   71

CHANSONS DE LUNE

La lune qui paraît   73
Deux lunes du soir   74
Lundi, mercredi, vendredi   76
Mort au petit matin   77
Premier anniversaire   78
Deuxième anniversaire   79
Fleur   80

ÉROS AVEC CANNE
(1925)

Frayeur dans la salle à manger   81
Lucia Martinez   82
La vieille fille à la messe   83
Intérieur   84
Nu   85
Sérénade   86
A Malaga   87

247

OUTREMONDE

Scène	89
Nuit et malaise	90
L'enfant muet	91
L'enfant fou	92
Fiançailles	93
Adieu	94
Suicide	95

AMOUR

Petit air du premier désir	97
Au lycée et à l'université	99
Petit madrigal	100
Écho	101
Idylle	102
Narcisse	103
Grenade en 1850	104
Prélude	105
Sur le vert du ciel	106
Sonnet	107

CHANSONS POUR FINIR

D'une autre façon	109
Chanson de novembre et d'avril	110
Onde, où t'en vas-tu?...	111
Le miroir trompeur	112
Chanson inutile	113
Verger de mars	114

Deux marins au bord de l'eau   115
Angoisse de statue   116
Chanson de l'oranger sec   117
Chanson du jour qui s'en va   118

POÈME DU CANTE JONDO

PETITE BALLADE DES TROIS RIVIÈRES   121

POÈME DE LA SÉGUIDILLE GITANE

Paysage   123
La guitare   124
Le cri   125
Le silence   126
Passage de la Séguidille   127
Après le passage   128
Et après   129

POÈME DE LA SOLEA

Terre sèche   131
Village   132
Poignard   133
Carrefour   134
Aïe !   135
Surprise   136
La Solea   137
Grotte   138

249

Rencontre   139
Aube   140

POÈME DE LA SAETA

Archers   141
Nuit   142
Séville   143
Procession   145
Paso   146
Saeta   147
Balcon   148
Petit jour   149

GRAPHIQUE DE LA PETENERA

Cloche   151
Chemin   152
Les six cordes   153
Danse   154
Mort de la petenera   155
Fausset   156
De profundis   157
Clameur   158

DEUX JEUNES FILLES

Lola   159
Amparo   160

VIGNETTES FLAMENCAS

Portrait de Silverio Franconetti 161
Juan Breva 162
Café-concert 163
Lamentation de la mort 164
Conjuration 166
Mémento 167

TROIS VILLES

Malaga 169
Quartier de Cordoue 170
Danse 171

SIX CAPRICES

Devinette de la guitare 173
Chaleil 174
Crotale 175
Cactus 176
Agave 177
Croix 178

SCÈNE DU LIEUTENANT-COLONEL DE LA GARDE CIVILE

Salle des Drapeaux 179
Chanson du gitan rossé 182

DIALOGUE D'AMER

Une campagne   183
Chanson de la mère d'Amer   188

ROMANCERO GITAN

Romance de la lune, lune   191
Précieuse et le vent   193
La rixe   196
Romance somnambule   198
La nonne gitane   202
La femme adultère   204
Romance de la peine noire   207
Saint Michel (Grenade)   209
Saint Raphaël (Cordoue)   212
Saint Gabriel (Séville)   215
Prise d'Antoñito el Camborio sur la route de Séville 218
Mort d'Antoñito el Camborio   220
Mort d'amour   223
Romance de l'assigné   226
Romance de la Garde civile espagnole   229

TROIS ROMANCES HISTORIQUES

Le Martyre de sainte Eulalie   235
Romance burlesque de Don Pierre à cheval   238
Thamar et Amnon   241

DU MÊME AUTEUR

dans la même collection

POÉSIES I : Livre de poèmes, Mon village, *extraits* d'Impressions et paysages. *Traduction d'André Belamich et Claude Couffon.*

POÉSIE III : Poète à New York, Chant funèbre pour Ignacio Sanchez Mejias, Divan du Tamarit *et autres textes. Préface d'André Belamich. Traduction d'André Belamich, Pierre Darmangeat, Claude Couffon et Bernard Sesé.*

POÉSIES IV : Suites. Sonnets de l'amour obscur. *Préface et traduction d'André Belamich.*

DERNIÈRES PARUTIONS

231. ***   Chansonnier révolutionnaire.
232. ***   Anthologie de la poésie lyrique fran-
                                    çaise des XIIᵉ et XIIIᵉ siècles.
233. Daniel Boulanger   Tchadiennes.
234. René Char   Éloge d'une Soupçonnée.
235. Henri Michaux   La vie dans les plis.
236. Robert Sabatier   Les châteaux de millions d'années.
237. Norge   Poésies 1923-1988.
238. Octavio Paz   Le feu de chaque jour.
239. Claude Roy   À la lisière du temps.
240. Edmond Jabès   Le Seuil Le Sable.
241. Pierre Louÿs   Les Chansons de Bilitis.
242. Miguel Angel Asturias   Poèmes indiens.
243. Georg Trakl   Crépuscule et déclin.
244. Henri Michaux   Misérable miracle.
245. Guillevic   Étier suivi de Autres.
246. Adonis   Mémoire du vent.
247. Max Jacob   Poèmes de Morven le Gaélique.
248. Dylan Thomas   Vision et Prière.
249. ***   Chansons françaises de la Renais-
                                    sance.
250. Eugenio Montale   Poèmes choisis (1916-1980).
251. Herman Melville   Poèmes de guerre.
252. André du Bouchet   Dans la chaleur vacante.
253. Gaspara Stampa   Poèmes.
254. Daniel Boulanger   Intailles.

255.	Martial	*Épigrammes.*
256.	Michel-Ange	*Poèmes.*
257.	John Donne	*Poèmes.*
258.	Henri Michaux	*Face aux verrous.*
259.	William Faulkner	*Le Faune de marbre. Un rameau vert.*
260.	Walt Whitman	*Poèmes.*
261.	Stéphane Mallarmé	*Poésies.*
262.	Yves Bonnefoy	*Rue Traversière.*
263.	***	*Anthologie de la poésie française du XIXᵉ siècle, II.*
264.	Hugo von Hofmannsthal	*Lettre de Lord Chandos.*
265.	Paul Valéry	*Ego scriptor.*
266.	Goethe	*Élégie de Marienbad.*
267.	Lorand Gaspar	*Égée. Judée.*
268.	Jacques Réda	*Les Ruines de Paris.*
269.	Jude Stéfan	*À la Vieille Parque.*
270.	Rainer Maria Rilke	*Lettres à un jeune poète.*
271.	Pierre Torreilles	*Denudare.*
272.	Friedrich Hölderlin	*Odes. Élégies. Hymnes.*
273.	W.B. Yeats	*Quarante-cinq poèmes.*
274.	Bernard Noël	*La Chute des temps.*
275.	***	*Anthologie de la poésie russe.*
276.	André Chénier	*Poésies.*
277.	Philippe Jaccottet	*À la lumière d'hiver.*
278.	Daniel Boulanger	*Hôtel de l'image.*
279.	Charles Leconte de Lisle	*Poèmes antiques.*
280.	Alexandre Pouchkine	*Poésies.*
281.	Elizabeth Browning	*Sonnets portugais.*
282.	Henri Michaux	*L'infini turbulent.*
283.	Rainer Maria Rilke	*Élégies de Duino. Sonnets à Orphée.*
284.	Maurice Blanchard	*Les Barricades mystérieuses.*
285.	Omar Khayam	*Rubayat.*
286.	Agrippa d'Aubigné	*Les Tragiques.*
287.	Jean Cassou	*Trente-trois sonnets composés au secret.*
288.	***	*La planche de vivre.*
289.	Pierre Jean Jouve	*Dans les années profondes.*
290.	John Milton	*Le Paradis perdu.*

291. Pablo Neruda — *La Centaine d'amour.*
292. Yves Bonnefoy — *Ce qui fut sans lumière.*
293. Pier Paolo Pasolini — *Poèmes de jeunesse.*
294. Jacques Audiberti — *Ange aux entrailles.*
295. Henri Pichette — *Apoèmes.*
296. Stéphane Mallarmé — *Vers de circonstance.*
297. John Keats — *Poèmes et poésies.*
298. Paul Claudel — *Cent phrases pour éventails.*
299. Louis Calaferte — *Rag-time.*
300. André Breton — *Poisson soluble.*
301. David Herbert Lawrence — *Poèmes.*
302. *** — *Les poètes du Chat Noir.*
303. Joachim Du Bellay — *Divers Jeux rustiques.*
304. Juvénal — *Satires.*
305. Odysseus Elytis — *Axion Esti.*
306. Nuno Júdice — *Un chant dans l'épaisseur du temps.*
307. Pentti Holappa — *Les mots longs.*
308. Max Elskamp — *La Chanson de la rue Saint-Paul.*
309. *** — *Anthologie de la poésie religieuse française.*
310. René Char — *En trente-trois morceaux.*
311. Friedrich Nietzsche — *Poèmes (1858-1888). Dithyrambes pour Dionysos.*
312. Daniel Boulanger — *Les dessous du ciel.*

Ce volume,
le deuxième de la collection Poésie,
a été achevé d'imprimer sur les presses
de l'imprimerie Bussière à Saint-Amand (Cher),
le 3 juillet 1997.
Dépôt légal : juillet 1997.
1ᵉʳ dépôt légal dans la collection : février 1966.
Numéro d'imprimeur : 1432.
ISBN 2-07-030170-2./Imprimé en France.

The Pocket Essential

GEORGES SIMENON

www.pocketessentials.com

First published in Great Britain 2003 by
Pocket Essentials, P O Box 394, Harpenden, Herts, AL5 1XJ, UK

Distributed in the USA by Trafalgar Square Publishing,
PO Box 257, Howe Hill Road, North Pomfret, Vermont 05053

Copyright © David Carter 2003
Series Editor: David Mathew

A CIP catalogue record for this book is available from the British Library.

ISBN 1-904048-21-8

2 4 6 8 10 9 7 5 3 1

Book typeset by Wordsmith Solutions Ltd
Printed and bound by Cox & Wyman

For Kim Chan Young
and his family

Acknowledgements

In the first place I must recognise an enormous debt to scholars who have laboured in the field of Simenon studies before me. My own researches have been checked constantly against theirs. There is no scope however in this modest volume for detailed citation of sources. I am also greatly indebted to the advice and help of Christine Swings-Deliege of the Centre for Simenon Studies and the Fonds Simenon at the University of Liège, to the staff of the British Film Institute archives in London, of the BBC, Penguin Books UK, and of Harcourt Brace Jovanovich, USA. For checking details of filmographies I am grateful to William J. Arrowsmith and Tony Pratt. Obscurities in the French language were clarified for me by Philip and Bénédicte Morris. Graham Cranfield, Head of the Humanities Reference Service at the British Library, helped me in many ways, and he and his wife Margaret also lent me several volumes from 'The Cranfield Simenon Collection'. I am also very grateful to Dennis Burton, for loans from his Simenon collection, and for the countless stimulating discussions on Simenon we have had over the years.

CONTENTS

1. Introduction: From Romance To Realism.................7
Note on the Checklists

2. The Life And The Legend 9

3. The Maigret Works 14
Origins
Development Of The Maigret Series
Checklist Of All Maigret Works

4. The 'Romans Durs'....................................48
Checklist of 'Romans Durs'

5. Simenon On Film......................................79
Maigret on Film
'Romans Durs' on Film

6. Simenon On TV And Radio.....................91
Maigret on TV
BBC Radio Four Maigret Series

7. Reference Materials 93
Simenon Editions
Biographies
Bibliography
Institutions And Societies
Internet Resources

1. Introduction: From Romance To Realism

It is difficult, in retrospect, to determine which is the earlier memory: holding a slim, immaculate, and stylish green and white Penguin volume in my hands, or watching the first BBC TV Maigret with Rupert Davies. I was studying French at school, never having been to France, and was familiar with all the romantic, Bohemian imagery associated with Paris: artists, steep alleys, iron-railed steps, art nouveau metro entrances, big cups of coffee, croissants and accordions. I think that the Penguin covers might just have got to me before Rupert Davies did, but the two are blended in my memory. And Ron Grainer's haunting theme music, with its climax timed so well with Rupert Davies' striking of a match on a lamp-lit wall, confirmed the birth of a life-long love affair.

If it started with romance it ended with realities. That first BBC TV series was justifiably praised. Here was a crime series that went against all one had assumed were the rules of crime fiction. There were twists and turns of plot, but one could often guess, at least as early as Maigret did, who the murderer was. Here was no planting of ingenious clues, no Sherlock Holmes or Hercule Poirot. Not even a Miss Marple! Here in fact were not 'whodunits' at all. If anything they were 'whydunits.' If Maigret has genius it is for intuitive understanding. He understands by soaking himself in atmosphere, comprehending a lifestyle, discovering people's emotional and physical needs. For a teenager it was a revelation. I had never believed a detective story could reveal such depths.

From watching the TV Maigrets (either the BBC TV series or the recent Granada TV series, with Michael Gambon), many people turned to the original novels. When I read Simenon's works in French I was also pleased to discover that his simple, clear style seemed to have lost little in translation. Some noticeable stylistic features undoubtedly have their roots in his earlier pseudonymous writings for popular magazines, but he refined them into highly expressive techniques. The first very obvious feature is the prevalence of very short paragraphs, containing at most two or three sentences, and some only one. Yet a locality, a house, an atmosphere is very vividly conjured up by the careful choice of telling detail. Following Colette's advice ("Get rid of all the literature, and it will be alright") Simenon also simplified his language and claimed to have used a vocabulary of no more than 2,000 words. A device he also used to frequently arresting effect, is the unanswerable question. As distinct from the questions, which characters ask themselves and to which answers are in principle ascertainable, there is occasionally a probing, altogether more profound question, to which no simple answer is provided. One impressive example is to be found near the beginning of the novel *Ticket Of*

Leave, when the widow arrives at her house with the young ex-convict, who later becomes her lover. The question is posed but not answered: 'What made her notice some grease on the table-top?'

Many have discovered Simenon not through Maigret novels but through film versions of his novels. Most notable in recent years have been the adaptations of *Monsieur Hire* and *The Watchmaker of St Paul* (a version of *The Watchmaker of Everton*). More dedicated film lovers will recall also *Stranger In The House* (with James Mason) and *The Cat* (with Jean Gabin and Simone Signoret).

Until now there has been no handy work to guide the reader through his immense output. It is hoped that this slim volume will serve the needs not only of committed fans as a useful source of reference, but also of those who feel, rightly, that they have been missing out on a unique and brilliant writer all these years. He was one of the most prolific writers that the world has known. He wrote just under 200 novels in his own name, over 200 under eighteen pseudonyms, many volumes of short stories, several autobiographies, and dictated twenty-two volumes of memoirs. At one time he was one of the best-selling authors in the world, with over 500 million copies of his books available in 55 languages. The checklists of works in the present volume also include brief publishing histories, to aid readers in finding editions of works.

Harvest, USA, and Penguin are reissuing a selection of the Maigret novels in 2003, but on the occasion of the centenary of Simenon's birth (February 12th, 1903), it is high time to reprint some of the major works of this writer, whom André Gide described as 'the most genuine novelist we have had in literature'.

Note On The Checklists

In the checklists in chapters 3 and 4 only those novels translated into English are listed, by their first known English title but in the chronological order of their first publication in French. The original French title and date of publication are included in brackets. This is followed by details of the first British edition, with publisher and date, and of the first Penguin editions, including any variant titles, together with any available information on American editions. As many works are not at present in print this information is indispensable in tracking down copies. Publication histories are not comprehensive, as many works of Simenon's have not yet been translated.

The vast majority of the works are novels, and the reader should assume that a work is a novel unless otherwise indicated. Generally I have not revealed the ending of the novels so as to avoid spoiling the enjoyment of new readers.

2 The Life And The Legend

Simenon wrote two novels which are very autobiographical, though he did not want them to be considered as such: *Les trois crimes de mes amis* (not translated, but meaning 'The Three Crimes Of My Friends') and *Pedigree*. He also wrote four actual autobiographies and dictated twenty-two volumes of memoirs, after he had finally decided to stop writing novels. But all these works have to be read with a careful cross checking of the facts.

What is certain is that Georges Joseph Christian Simenon was born in Liège, Belgium on the February 12th, 1903. His father was Desiré Simenon (1876-1920), an insurance clerk. The Simenons had come to Liège originally from the district of Limburg and were French-speaking Walloons. Georges' mother, Henriette, née Brüll, had Dutch and German ancestry.

His relationship with his mother remained problematic throughout his life. He despised her as a fawning, small-minded woman, always concerned to keep up appearances with the neighbours.

In contrast to his depiction of his mother, he idealised his father. He admired his patience and his refusal to complain about his failures. A younger brother, Christian, firmly alienated Georges from his mother. It was clear that Christian was now favoured over Georges. The family was Catholic, and a large part of Simenon's childhood was devoted to church ritual.

At the beginning of the First World War, Simenon was still apparently a devout Catholic, but the wartime German occupation of Liège had a profound effect on him. He learned quickly that in order to survive in such times everyone had to deceive and cheat people. Signs of deviant behaviour started to appear in Simenon. He was more often to be seen in the town than at school and had started committing petty criminal offences.

The most disturbing event of Simenon's teenage years was the sudden and unexpected illness of his father. He had a heart condition, angina pectoris, which was incurable at that time. It seems that this event persuaded Simenon to leave school and earn a living to support his family. He went through various jobs, before he landed the post of journalist. He was employed at first, in January 1919, as an office boy and then as junior reporter with the *Gazette de Liège*, so that from the start he regarded himself as a professional writer. He wrote under several pseudonyms, settling for Georges Sim, which he retained for the next 12 years. As a journalist he learned skills which were to serve him well later as a novelist: he had to write quickly and meet deadlines. Despite his later denials that he had ever studied police methods, it is known that in this period he attended some lectures in his free time on developments in forensic medicine.

9

At this time he did something that was to prove of considerable embarrassment to him in later years. He wrote a series of anti-Semitic articles. He later explained that they were commissioned articles, and he had had no choice in the matter.

At this time too he was starting to write his first novels, which were not successful, and he was indulging in a Bohemian lifestyle. 'La Caque' ('The Herring Barrel') they called themselves, a small group of artistically-minded young men, who met nightly in a bar called 'L'Âne Rouge'. They met, often in a loft, to talk and read aloud the works of some writers, such as Friedrich Nietzsche. They reacted against conventional morality, the very notions of good and evil.

One symbol, which was adopted by 'La Caque', was that of the hanged man. It featured in the paintings of some of its members. One young friend, Kleine, a poor painter, was to become the victim of some of the most nihilistic aspects of the group's ideas; this was to haunt Simenon and feed a guilt complex for years to come. One night Kleine became very drunk and some members of the group carried him back to his room. The next morning Kleine was found dead, hanging from the door of St. Pholien's Church. The circumstances were suspicious and murder was suspected. Years later Simenon wrote '…We did not know the true state of Little Kleine. But in the last resort, wasn't it us who killed him?' One year after the event Simenon used the basic idea in the second Maigret novel, *Maigret And The Hundred Gibbets* (the French title of which means 'The Hanged Man Of St. Pholien').

While he was still a member of 'La Caque' Simenon met Régine Renchon, who was to become his first wife. He nicknamed her 'Tigy'. Older and more experienced, she was the dominant force in their relationship.

His father died in 1921, and after doing his military service he set off in December 1922 for Paris, where he worked as a secretary, first to Henri Binet-Valmer and then to the Marquis de Tracy. From 1923 to 1939 he gradually managed to establish himself as a pulp fiction writer. By 1931 he had produced about 200 novels and more than 1,000 short stories. He published these under 29 pseudonyms and catered for all ages and tastes.

In 1925 he and Tigy went on holiday near the port of Etretat, in Normandy, where he met Henriette Liberge, the eighteen-year-old daughter of a local fisherman. The couple persuaded her to come and work as Tigy's maid. Simenon promptly re-christened her 'Boule'. She was later to become his mistress.

In 1927 he started his affair with Josephine Baker. This fiery nineteen-year-old coloured singer and dancer from St. Louis was the sensation of Paris between 1925 and 1928. As a result of this Simenon wrote very little in 1927: only one collection of short stories and eleven popular pulp novels. After fleeing Josephine Baker's influence he managed to raise his production rate again in 1928 to forty-four novels for that year. But this period was not one of spent passion. He also made the acquaintance of the film director Jean Renoir and the painter Maurice de Vlaminck, with whom he developed a lasting friendship.

In the spring of 1928 he bought a boat, the *Ginette*, and he, Tigy and Boule set off for six months of travelling around France. By this time Simenon and Boule had become lovers. In 1929 he had a boat specially built for him, the *Ostrogoth*, and they travelled, Simenon writing all the while, to the Netherlands, other parts of Europe, and Scandinavia, including Norway and Lapland. It was probably on his return to Paris that the first true Maigret novel was written, and not in Holland, as Simenon claimed (see also chapter 3).

By April 1932 Simenon and his entourage had moved to a sixteenth-century mansion near La Rochelle. Being fairly well off by now, Simenon and Tigy decided to take a trip to Africa, though it was to be paid for by journalism. Simenon saw and experienced many things that confirmed his anti-colonialist views. Several of his exotically set novels have their roots in this trip.

In 1933 he wrote what he intended to be the last Maigret novel, *Maigret Returns*. By then he had also published six novels which he considered more literary in style, and which he called 'romans durs'.

In the same year he and Tigy undertook another trip around Europe, including a stay in Berlin, where Simenon happened to share a lift with an ordinary looking little man with a small square moustache: Adolf Hitler. They continued through Poland, Czechoslovakia, Hungary and Romania

In March 1934 there were problems with their lease for the property near La Rochelle, and they had to leave it. They spent the summer cruising on the Mediterranean, and in January 1935 he and Tigy set out on a world tour that was to last eight months. During this time he only produced one novel, during a stay on Tahiti. In January 1938 Simenon did something highly uncharacteristic of him: he joined a pacifist political movement.

When Germany invaded Holland and Belgium Simenon was called up to join a unit in Belgium, but the Belgian embassy appointed him Commissioner for Belgian Refugees. He was given full authority and financial support to help all Belgian refugees coming into the La Rochelle area.

Towards the end of 1940, after a consultation with a radiologist, Simenon was told that his heart was in an advanced state of decay, and that he might have at the most two years live. To channel his despair he wrote an autobiographical novel and a memoir called *Je me souviens* (never translated, but meaning 'I Remember'). André Gide and Simenon had been in correspondence with each other since 1938. It was on Gide's advice that Simenon fictionalised *Je me souviens* and it became the novel *Pedigree*.

Shortly after the Liberation, in 1944, Tigy discovered for the first time in fifteen years that Boule and her husband were lovers, and henceforth they kept their marriage together only for the sake of their son Marc. In 1945 Simenon left France with Tigy and Marc for America via England.

Within a few weeks of arriving in New York in October 1945, Simenon met and started an affair with Denyse Ouimet, a 25-year-old French Canadian, who eventually became his second wife. In keeping with his usual habit Simenon changed her name (albeit slightly) and called her Denise.

After a brief trip to Cuba in January 1947 with Denise, the group settled in Tucson, Arizona. It was here, in 1948, that he wrote one of the novels regarded by many as a masterpiece: *The Snow Was Black*. Boule now joined them from France. In January 1949 Denise announced that she was pregnant. Tigy, Boule and Marc then went to live in California. When his son John was born, Simenon and Denise also went to live in California, in Carmel-by-the-Sea, mainly to be near Marc. Finally Simenon was divorced from Tigy and married Denise on two successive days in Reno, Nevada. While he was living in California Simenon made a visit to Hollywood. He met Charlie Chaplin, who remained a friend and later became his neighbour in Switzerland. Most significantly he renewed his acquaintance with Jean Renoir.

In September 1950 Simenon and Denise moved to Shadow Rock Farm at Lakeville, Connecticut. In 1952 he was made a member of the Belgian Académie Royale, and in the next year his only daughter, Marie-Jo, was born.

Suddenly, in March 1955, Simenon decided to return to Europe, and after they had settled near Cannes, Denise suffered a miscarriage. Finally they took up residence in the Swiss canton of Vaud and bought a château near Lausanne. In 1961 they had a new maid, Teresa Sburelin, who, in the Simenon tradition, eventually became his mistress.

The next ten years of his life can only be described as tragic for Simenon. Denise had spent some time in psychiatric care in 1962, and she and Simenon moved to their new specially designed house at Epalinges in 1963. But the relationship was shattered, and Denise finally left Epalinges in 1964, followed later in the year by Boule. His cherished daughter, Marie-Jo, who also had psychiatric treatment in 1966, had suffered a complete nervous breakdown in 1970. (Eight years later, in 1978, in her Paris apartment, she commited suicide.) In December of 1970 his mother died. And in the following year Simenon changed his life radically. He wrote his last 'roman dur', *The Innocents*, and his last Maigret, *Maigret And Monsieur Charles*. The house at Epalinges was sold and he moved, with Teresa as companion and housekeeper, to a small apartment on the eighth floor in Lausanne.

In February 1973 he announced that he would write no more novels, and kept that promise. But six days later he started to dictate into a tape-recorder his memoirs, which amounted eventually to twenty-two volumes. Here he lived the life of a recluse, though he was enticed out occasionally, and most famously for the interview with his close friend Federico Fellini, in which he claimed to have made love to 10,000 women. Was this just another example of the old man confusing fact and fantasy? Or a reasonable estimate by a man who needed sexual intercourse more than once every day of his adult life?

Georges Simenon died at the age of 86 on September 4th, 1989, in Lausanne.

3. The Maigret Works

Origins

According to Simenon he was trying to write a detective story on his boat, the *Ostrogoth*, which was moored at the small Dutch port of Delfzijl, and wanted the story to be an improvement on the standard formulae for detective stories. He was sitting at a nearby café on a sunny morning, and in a rather drowsy state he imagined the big imposing figure of a man who would be suitable for a police inspector, and as the day wore on he had filled out the picture more: the man had a pipe, a heavy overcoat with a velvet collar and a bowler hat. And by noon the following day, he claimed, the first chapter of *The Case of Peter The Lett* had been written. Unfortunately it seems that it was not quite as simple as that.

What does appear to be certain is that Simenon wrote many stories and novels both in Delfzijl and another port, Stavoren, in Friesia, during this time, and that works he wrote on his barge in these places in 1929 were still detective pulp fiction. It is also possible that the novel *Train de nuit* under his pseudonym 'Christian Brull' was written in Delfzijl. It features a police inspector called Maigret. It seems likely that *The Case Of Peter the Lett* was actually written in Paris in the late spring or summer of 1930, but it was the first fully-fledged Maigret novel to be written in the style and with the ambience that one associates with the other famous Maigret novels. It is not without its antecedents however, in which the figure of a bulky inspector became progressively individualised. There were several 'Proto-Maigret' novels, written under various pseudonyms.

In the novel *L'aimant sans nom* (*The Nameless Lover,* as Christian Brulls,1929) there is a policeman known as No.49 who bears some resemblance to Maigret in his dogged questioning. And in a novel called *Fièvre* (*Fever,* as Brulls, 1932), which, although not published until 1932, was probably written much earlier, there is a burly chief inspector who behaves very much like Maigret, but Simenon gave him the name Torrence, which he later used for one of Maigret's inspectors. This Torrence gets involved emotionally with the criminal he is after, likes fishing and has a wife at home who always seems to have a nice meal waiting for him.

In *Train de nuit* (*Night Train,* as Brulls, 1929) a chief inspector called Maigret also appears. He is a member of the Marseilles police brigade, but does little more than direct operations and conduct a manhunt. He does reveal sympathy however for the destitute and is indulgent towards some of the criminals whom he considers to be victims of their situation.

In *La figurante* (*The Extra,* as Brulls, 1929) there is even a chapter headed 'The Impatience of Chief Inspector Maigret'. In this novel Maigret undertakes a real investigation, though in a somewhat passive manner. During an interrogation Maigret is described as being 'both gruff and paternal', and to one character he declares: 'Don't you realize that I am not concerned about you just as a police officer but as a human being?' He also retorts to a colleague in a typical Maigret manner: 'I don't believe! I don't think anything!' He is described as being 'huge and broad with a powerful neck'. And there are several references to his smoking a pipe.

In *La maison de l'inquiétude* (*A House Full Of Anxiety*, as Georges Sim, about 1929-30) the figure of Maigret is more the centre of attention, and his whole investigation is followed through from beginning to end. He belongs to the 'Brigade Mobile', is 'enormous and heavy', has 'large hands' and 'big fingers'. Also his fists are described a being like 'clubs'. He also wears a 'large dark overcoat' with 'a velvet collar' and sports a bowler hat. He has a pipe but breaks it in a fight, and is generally grumpy and impolite, but he sympathises readily with the victim. He also has the waiter in the local 'Brasserie des Orfèvres' bring up beers to his office. This is an obvious predecessor to the 'Brasserie Dauphine'. He lives on the Boulevard Richard-Lenoir, returns home to lunch, and has a 45 year-old wife. There is an Inspector Torrence and an Examining Magistrate Coméliau. The concierge in the house where Maigret makes enquiries has a yellow dog! A dog of the same hue features prominently in an early Maigret of 1931, *A Face For A Clue* (*Le chien jaune*, 1931). There is yet another character who seems to prefigure Maigret in *La femme rousse* (*The Redhead*, as Sim, written earlier but not published till 1933) but he plays a minor role compared to an Inspector Torrence.

Development Of The Maigret Series

Simenon's main publisher at the time, Fayard, took a lot of convincing that the new concept of detective novel would sell. In 1930 Simenon wrote four more Maigrets and agreed to produce a further five, so that in 1931 Fayard could launch the series with ten books. The first two actually published in 1931 were *The Death Of Monsieur Gallet* and *Maigret And The Hundred Gibbets*.

In this first series of Maigret novels, the total Maigret world is already established. All of the main characters are there, and the common settings. One feature of Maigret's personality is also fixed from the start: he never judges the criminals he pursues, and he often forsakes an arrest. It must be said that some of the characterization in the early Maigrets, especially that of minor characters, is akin to caricature, being broadly and brashly drawn.

Many fans prefer the earlier Maigrets and feel that the later ones are more philosophical and expansive. In the later ones however Simenon often attained greater subtlety of character and insight into motivation. And even the break, after the publication of *Maigret Returns*, in 1934, and lasting until the publication of three new novels in one volume in 1942, was not as complete a break as many have assumed. Since about 1936 Simenon had been continuing to write detective stories, and several of these featured Maigret. All were later to be published collectively in English in the volume *Maigret's Pipe*.

Simenon often downplayed the importance of the Maigret novels for him, but it is also true that he needed to write Maigrets. Over a period of twenty-six years he wrote fifty-three more Maigret novels, compared with only sixty 'romans durs', which means that the Maigrets made up almost half his creative output.

Checklist Of All Maigret Works

1) The Death Of Monsieur Gallet

(*M. Gallet décédé,* 1931). In *Introducing Inspector Maigret* (Hurst, 1933). Translated as *Maigret Stonewalled* (Penguin 2026, 1963), which is also included in the volume of three novels *Maigret At The Crossroads* (Penguin 6652, 1983).

Plot: The body of Emile Gallet is discovered in a hotel in Sancerre. Maigret is intrigued by the fact that he seems to have been leading a double life. It turns out that Gallet was not the sales representative that everyone took him to be, but a crook who had discovered ways in which he could blackmail certain wealthy individuals, and one rich lord in particular: Tiburce de Saint-Hilaire. Gallet himself however became a victim of blackmail, and devised an insurance scam to benefit his own wife. The final truth that Maigret uncovers involves a remarkable twist.

Comments: The novel, which is one of the earliest Maigrets to be written, has scenes set not only in Sancerre but also in Paris and the Ile-de-France. It is clearly based on Simenon's experience of meeting a group of French loyalists after his first arrival in Paris from Belgium. There are numerous twists and turns in the plot, which are reminiscent of the conventions of the popular novels he had been writing hitherto. 4/5

2) The Crime of Inspector Maigret

(*Le pendu de Saint-Pholien,* 1931). In *Introducing Inspector Maigret* (Hurst, 1933). Translated as *Maigret And The Hundred Gibbets* (Penguin 2025, 1963), which is also included in the volume of three novels *Maigret Meets A Milord* (Penguin 6651, 1983).

Plot: Maigret gets involved, almost by chance, in investigating a murder that happened ten years previously. He becomes intrigued by the odd behaviour of someone he sees during a trip to Brussels. A rather shabby-looking man packs up some thousand-franc notes and posts them off as 'printed matter'. Maigret follows him to Bremen, Germany, and is present when he commits suicide. He discovers his identity and the fact that he had some connection with a rather suspicious group of individuals in Liège, who call themselves 'The Companions of the Apocalypse'. In this city Maigret learns that one of this group had killed another of the members during a nocturnal drinking session and then subsequently committed suicide. The man pursued by Maigret had started to blackmail his former comrades to gain revenge and, when proof of his activities is uncovered by Maigret, he in turn decides to commit suicide. The ending reveals Maigret at his most human and forgiving.

Comments: Some critics have found the plot a little far-fetched, but in fact it is very closely based on events in Simenon's own life. He belonged to a similar group called 'La Caque' when he lived in Liège. A member of the group died in mysterious circumstances. It looked like suicide but some thought it had been murder. The young man's name was Kleine; in the novel it is Klein. Whatever the truth of the matter, Simenon's fictional version involves a real murder. At the time there existed a law of 'prescription' in Belgium, by which one could not be prosecuted for a crime after a lapse of ten years, and it is this fact that determines Maigret's action at the end of the novel. The real life Kleine had died only eight years before the publication of the book, however, which must have made Simenon unpopular with his old friends. The book is worth reading for its atmosphere alone. 3/5

3) The Crime At Lock 14

(*Le charretier de 'La Providence'*, 1931). In *The Triumph Of Inspector Maigret* (Hurst, 1934). Translated as *Maigret Meets A Milord* (Penguin 2027, 1963), which is also included in the volume of three novels *Maigret Meets A Milord* (Penguin 6651, 1983).

Plot: A woman's body is discovered near a lock in the vicinity of Epernay. The husband of the victim, Sir Walter Lampson, who is the owner of a yacht, and his companions are under immediate suspicion. The occupants of a mysterious barge also seem to have some connection with the crime. A friend of the lord, Willy Marco, is also murdered and the carter, Jean, has an accident. Maigret finds himself somewhat at a loss but finally manages to solve the mystery when he delves into the background of the carter (who is referred to in the title of the original French novel).

Comments: It is a very accomplished novel, in which Maigret reveals clearly his understanding of human suffering, and it is memorable also for its evocation of dull rainy weather along the canals and the atmosphere of towpath cafés. 5/5

4) A Face For A Clue

(*Le chien jaune*, 1931). In *The Patience Of Maigret* (Routledge, 1939; Harcourt, USA, 1940). Also in *A Crime In Holland And A Face For A Clue* (Penguin 856, 1952).

Plot: Maigret goes to the old town of Concarneau to investigate the attempted murder of a prominent person. Just after his arrival another regular visitor to the Hôtel de l'Amiral disappears in mysterious circumstances and a third is poisoned. Maigret decides to put the surviving partner of the three men, Dr. Michoux, in jail, for his own safety. While all this is happening a mysterious dog with yellow fur (referred to in the French title) is found roaming around the district. The local authorities become rather anxious at Maigret's apparent inaction. He however is intrigued by the behaviour of the waitress, Emma, at the hotel, who also seems to have a relationship with Léon, the owner of the yellow dog. Maigret finally discovers that at the heart of the mystery there is a drug peddling racket.

Comments: This became one of the most well known of the early Maigrets due to the fact that it was filmed within a year of its first publication. 4/5

5) The Case Of Peter The Lett

(*Pietr-le-Letton*, 1931). In *Inspector Maigret Investigates* (Hurst, 1933). Translated as *Maigret And The Enigmatic Lett* (Penguin 2023, 1963), which is also included in *Maigret Meets A Milord* (Penguin 6651, 1983).

Plot: The police are expecting the arrival in Paris of the crook known as Peter the Lett. A body is dioscovered in a train at the Gare du Nord, which proves to be Peter's double. The real Peter has arrived but managed to escape police surveillance. Maigret manages to track him down, but it soon becomes a very personal case for him, when one of his inspectors, Torrence, is killed while keeping watch on the Lett. Then Maigret himself is wounded and a witness is killed. But Maigret soldiers on, more concerned to find the murderer than for his own health, and there is an unexpected twist at the end.

Comments: The plot has many surprising twists and turns, and Simenon is at times more judgemental than in his later writings. Some of the characterisation verges on caricature, lacking the subtlety he was too develop later. It is likely that this was the first fully-fledged Maigret novel to be written. Simenon himself always claimed it was the first Maigret. He finished the novel in the spring of 1930 and could only persuade his publisher, Arthème Fayard, to publish it on the condition that he would be able to publish several other Simenon titles at the same time. This is why a whole batch of Maigrets appeared in the same year. The novel is also remarkable for the fact that the author killed off one of Maigret's inspectors, Torrence, so early in the series. He was of course very quickly revived. 3/5

6) The Crossroad Murders

(*La nuit du carrefour*, 1931). In *Inspector Maigret Investigates* (Hurst, 1933). Translated as *Maigret At The Crossroads* (Penguin 2028, 1963), which was also included in the volume of three novels *Maigret At The Crossroads* (Penguin 6652, 1983).

Plot: A diamond dealer from Anvers is found dead at the wheel of a car belonging to the insurance agent Michonnet at an isolated crossroads near Arpajon. Maigret discovers strange relationships linking the inhabitants of the three houses at the crossroads. There are the insurance agent and his wife, a Danish aristocrat, Carl Andersen, and his German wife Else, a former prostitute, and Oscar, the garage owner and former boxer. The mystery deepens when the wife of the diamond dealer is also killed and the aristocrat is seriously wounded. Maigret himself also narrowly escapes an attempt on his life. He manages to establish that the garage owner is involved in some shady dealings. The resolution sees justice done but love triumphant.

Comments: The central focus of the novel is on the former prostitute Else. The unusual setting also adds to the work's fascination. It became very well known after Jean Renoir's film version made in 1932. 4/5

7) A Crime In Holland

(*Un crime en Hollande*, 1931). In *Maigret Abroad* (Routledge, 1940;Harcourt, USA, 1940). Also in *A Crime In Holland And A Face For A Clue* (Penguin 856, 1952).

Plot: Maigret is sent to the little Dutch village of Delfzijl to investigate the murder of Conrad Popinga, a local teacher, because a Frenchman, Jean Duclos, who was a guest of Popinga's, seems to be involved in the affair and it was he who in fact discovered the weapon. But among the suspects are the victim's mistress, Beetje, a rejected lover, an old sailor, Popinga's actual wife, his sister-in-law, Any, a lawyer, and a frightened cadet. Maigret gradually eliminates various false leads to arrive at the truth, but has a crisis of conscience when the murderer commits suicide.

Comments: The novel is not short of suspects and intriguing clues (a sailor's hat in a bathtub and a cigar butt).The unraveling of the mystery is not so fascinating however as the evocation of the conservative nature of bourgeois life and its values in a small Dutch town. Light and atmosphere are very well conveyed. It is also memorable for Maigret's own reflections on the responsibilities of the investigator. 3/5

8) The Sailor's Rendez-vous

(*Au rendez-vous des Terre-Neuvas*, 1931). In *Maigret Keeps A Rendez-vous* (Routledge, 1940; Harcourt, USA, 1941). Also under the same title in Penguin 3136, 1970.

Plot: Captain Fallut is discovered strangled in a pool in the port of Fécamp. A young telegraph operator, who was prowling around his boat, is immediately under suspicion. Maigret is contacted by a friend of his, who is a local primary school teacher, and he sets out to prove the innocence of the young man, Le Clinche. He discovers that the captain was hiding his mistress, Adele, on board the trawler, which roused the jealousy of both the telegraph operator and the chief engineer, who had discovered what the captain was up to. But a young ship's apprentice also discovered the captain's secret, and it was his threat to reveal all to the ship's crew that led to a series of tragic events culminating in the captain's death.

Comments: The novel is memorable for its maritime setting and oppressive atmosphere. 4/5

9) A Battle Of Nerves

(*La tête d'un homme*, 1931). In *The Patience Of Maigret* (Routledge, 1939;Harcourt, USA, 1940). Also in *A Battle Of Nerves And At The 'Gai Moulin'* (Penguin 739, 1950). Translated as *Maigret's War Of Nerves* (Harcourt, USA, 1986).

Plot: Maigret does not believe that Joseph Heurtin, who has been condemned to death, is guilty of the double murder of Madame Henderson and her female companion. He therefore enables him to escape, and arranges to have him followed in the hope that this will help him to discover the real guilty parties. He encounters the victim's nephew, Crosby, and a Czech student, and eventually uncovers a complex plan to put the blame on the unsuspecting Heurtin. The true criminal is finally caught and condemned to death in Heurtin's place.

Comments: Unusually Maigret is allowed to correct a judicial error with the full support of the authorities. 4/5

10) At The Gai-Moulin

(*La danseuse du Gai-Moulin*, 1931). In *Maigret Abroad* (Routledge, 1940;Harcourt, USA, 1940). Also in *A Battle Of Nerves And At The Gai-Moulin* (Penguin 739, 1950).

Plot: Two young men, Delfosse and Chabot, deliberately allow themselves to be locked inside a nightclub called the 'Gai-Moulin' in Liège, with the intention of stealing the takings. In the darkness they stumble over a body and run off. The following day the body of one of the club's clientele, a Greek called Graphopolous, is discovered in a public garden. The investigation culminates in the arrest of the two young men and one other suspect, who turns out to be none other than Maigret, who had been following the victim. He allows himself to be arrested by the Belgian police before revealing his true identity. The two young men are set free and Maigret investigates the role of Adèle, a dancer at the club, who seems to be involved in the affair and who leads him to the solution of the mystery.

Comments: In this novel Maigret makes one of his most surprising and dramatic entries. It is also fascinating for its depiction of Simenon's home town, Liège, and for its study of one of the young men, Jean Chabot, who resembles in many ways Simenon himself at that age, and who had also been tempted at one time into crime. 4/5

11) The Guingette By The Seine

(*La Guingette à Deux Sous*, 1932). In *Maigret To The Rescue* (Routledge, 1940; Harcourt, USA, 1941; Pan 138, 1950). Reissued under the title *Maigret And The Tavern By The Seine* (Harcourt Brace, USA, 1990).

Plot: On the eve of going to the guillotine, Jean Lenoir informs Maigret that he had been witness to a crime six years previously. He and his partner had witnessed someone dumping a body into a canal. Lenoir subsequently blackmailed the murderer, who managed to disappear and was not seen again until one evening at a tavern by the Seine, the 'Guingette à Deux Sous'. Maigret goes to the tavern to investigate and mingles with local people and customers in this peaceful spot. He also meets up with a merry band of Parisians: James, Basso and Mado and Marcel Feinstein. But their gaiety is short-lived when one of them is murdered. Maigret also manages to find Lenoir's accomplice, Victor, and learns the name of the man who was killed six years before. It was a usurer called Ulrich. Maigret realizes that he is in fact unraveling two crimes.

Comments: There may be some surprising coincidences in the novel but it skillfully weaves together two interrelated plotlines and reveals yet again Maigret's ambiguous attitude towards the criminal. 5/5

12) The Shadow In The Courtyard

(*L'ombre chinoise*, 1932). In *The Triumph Of Inspector Maigret* (Hurst, 1934). Translated as *Maigret Mystified* (Penguin 2024, 1964), which was also included in the volume of three novels *Maigret At The Crossroads* (Penguin 6652, 1983).

Plot: Raymond Couchet has been murdered in his office in the Place des Vosges and a significant sum of money has been stolen. Maigret questions his first wife, Juliette Martin, their son Roger, his mistress Nina and also keeps an eye on his widow. Roger commits suicide and this event leads to the revelation of what really happened, with the culprit unable to cope and descending into madness.

Comments: One of the attractions of this novel is the blending of three different locales: there are scenes in the world of petty officials, in that of the higher levels of the bourgeoisie and in the area around Pigalle. Simenon lived in the Place des Vosges at one time and knew it well. 5/5

13) The Saint-Fiacre Affair

(*L'affaire Saint-Fiacre*, 1932). In *Maigret Keeps A Rendez-Vous* (Routledge, 1940; Harcourt, USA, 1941). Translated as *Maigret Goes Home* (Penguin 1901, 1967).

Plot: The police at Moulins receive a message informing them that a crime will be committed in the church at Saint-Fiacre during the first mass on All Souls' Day. When Maigret learns of this he decides to be there on that day. One reason for his interest is that it is the place where he was born and he had spent his childhood by the château, for which his father had been estate manager. He attends the mass on that day and watches the old countess, who, he suddenly realizes, is dead. She has died from shock at seeing a false report in a newspaper announcing the death of her son Maurice. The investigation focuses on the immediate entourage of the countess: the son, who always seems to need money, Jean Métayer, the secretary and lover of the countess, and Gautier, the estate manager and his son. The crime, and its motive, are finally unraveled during a dinner party organized by Maurice.

Comments: This novel is well known among Maigret fans, because of the biographical details revealed about the inspector's childhood. The novel concludes without the intervention of the law. 4/5

14) The Flemish Shop

(*Chez les Flamands*, 1932). In *Maigret To The Rescue* (Routledge, 1940; Harcourt, USA, 1941; Pan 138, 1950).

Plot: The daughter of a night watchman in Givet has disappeared. The young woman, Germaine Piedboeuf, has had a child by Joseph Peeters. She never found acceptance among the group of Flemish people and there is a rumor that some rich shopkeepers arranged her disappearance. Maigret goes to Givet in a private capacity at the request of Anna Peeters. He gets to know Joseph, Anna's brother, Maria, his young sister, who is a primary school teacher, and his mother. It seems that the Peeters played no part in the affair. Germaine's body is found in the river Meuse, with the skull smashed in, and a bargeman is suspected of the crime. When he finally solves the crime, Maigret decides to keep quiet about it, because he has not been officially appointed to investigate it. He allows the real perpetrator to leave for Paris, while the bargeman is still at large.

Comments: The novel provides another example of Maigret dispensing his own justice and not acting within the confines of the law. 3/5

15) The Madman Of Bergerac

(*Le fou de Bergerac*, 1932). In *Maigret Travels South* (Routledge, 1940; Harcourt, USA, 1940; Penguin 826, 1952).

Plot: On his way to the Dordogne to take a holiday Maigret sees a man jump out of a train as it slows down. He immediately follows him and is wounded. While recovering in hospital in Bergerac he learns that there have been several crimes committed locally by someone suspected of being a madman, and realizes that he himself may have been attacked by the man. There is general panic in the town, and Maigret helps the local authorities from the confines of his hospital bed. The corpse of a man called Meyer is found in a wood, and Maigret decides to concentrate his investigation on a group of local dignitaries. This reveals the true identity of Meyer and the person who killed him.

Comments: The fact that Maigret undertakes the entire investigation from a hospital bed seems to emphasize his genius for intuition. 3/5

16) Death Of A Harbour Master

(*Le port des brumes*, 1932). In *Maigret And M. Labbe* (Routledge, 1941; Harcourt, USA, 1942).

Plot: A former merchant sea captain, and now harbour master at the small port of Oistreham on the English Channel, Yves Joris is found after he disappeared for seven weeks, but he has lost his memory. He has obviously been wounded and looked after. Maigret takes him back to Ouistreham, where the dies of strychnine poisoning just after his arrival. The inspector comes up against a wall of silence. Joris seems to have had some connection with a Norwegian who was born in France, Ernest Grandmaison, a rich shipowner and a former convict. Grandmaison's suicide prompts people to start talking. It seems that Joris had helped a criminal to escape and been wounded in the process. The person who wounded him feared being recognized by Joris and killed him.

Comments: A justly famous novel, with a memorable evocation of a foggy seaport. The fog becomes a metaphor for the cover-up of human motivations. 5/5

17) Liberty Bar

(*'Liberty Bar'*, 1932). In *Maigret Travels South* (Routledge, 1940; Harcourt, USA, 1940; Penguin 826, 1952).

Plot: An alcoholic Australian, William Brown, is stabbed to death in Antibes, on the French Riviera. Maigret attempts to reconstruct the events leading up to the crime, and meets his mistress, Gina, and her mother, Jaja, who owns the Liberty Bar. Here he also meets Sylvie, a young prostitute, and her pimp Joseph. He also encounters the victim's son, Harry, who is trying to track down a will. Not for the first time Maigret uncovers a double crime.

Prison is the just dessert in one case, but Maigret allows Brown's killer to go free. He has his reasons.

Comments: This novel is remarkable for its unusual setting on the Côte d'Azur. Maigret's sense of pity overrides his respect for the law. 4/5

18) The Lock At Charenton

(*L'écluse no.1*, 1933). In *Maigret Sits It Out* (Routledge, 1940; Harcourt, USA, 1940; Penguin 826, 1952).

Plot: Old Gassin falls off the gangway of his barge after a drunken evening. As he is trying to get out of the water, a man grabs hold of him. It is shipowner Emile Ducrau. When both men are finally fished out it is discovered that Ducrau has been stabbed and the police are alerted. Maigret concentrates especially on the background of Ducrau, and discovers that he is the father of Aline Gassin, a mentally retarded woman and the mother of a young boy. The tension mounts when Ducrau's son Jean commits suicide and an assistant lock-keeper is found hanged. The final confession brings with it a sense of release for the murderer.

Comments: The novel is rather disturbing due to the sordid nature of the relationships involved. 3/5

19) Maigret Returns

(*Maigret*, 1934). In *Maigret Sits It Out* (Routledge, 1941; Harcourt, USA, 1942; Penguin 827, 1952).

Plot: A certain Inspector Lauer, who is Maigret's nephew, is in a delicate professional situation. He was unable to prevent the murder of a man he had under surveillance, Pepito, the boss of a bar called the 'Floria.' What is more he is the prime suspect because of the way he panicked. While enjoying his retirement on the banks of the Loire, Maigret is visited by his nephew, who begs for his help. He agrees, but encounters difficulties with his former colleagues. It proves to have been a gangland killing to silence Pepito.

Comments: This novel is unique in the Maigret series, with the former chief inspector solving a crime in his retirement. Simenon in fact intended it to be the last of the series, and wanted to devote himself afterwards entirely to the writing of 'romans durs'. After 1933 he wrote no Maigret novels for five years, though he did write some Maigret short stories. 3/5

20) Maigret And The Spinster

(*Cécile est morte* in *Maigret Revient*, 1942). Hamilton, 1977; Harcourt, USA, 1977; in *The Fourteenth Simenon Omnibus*, (Penguin 4675, 1979); and Harvest 129, USA, 1982.

Plot: For six months Maigret has been visited frequently by a 28-year-old spinster, Cécile Pardon, who lives with her aunt, and is convinced that strangers have been regularly breaking into their house. No evidence is found to support her claims. But one day, when she is due to visit Maigret, she does not turn up. When Maigret goes to the house he finds that the two women have been strangled. During his investigations he brings to light the fact that the aunt was once the owner of a house of ill repute that was visited by some suspicious characters. One of these is a certain Charles Dandurand. It becomes clear that the same person did not murder both women.

Comments: Some critics have found the novel's plot confusing, but it also contains much of that haunting Parisian atmosphere that true aficionados relish. 4/5

21) Maigret And The Hotel Majestic

(*Les caves du Majestic*, in *Maigret Revient*, 1942). Hamilton, 1977; Harcourt, USA, 1978; Harvest 133, USA, 1982; and in the volume of three novels *Maigret And The Ghost* (Penguin 4676, 1982).

Plot: Maigret is asked to conduct a discreet investigation of the murder of an American woman, Mrs. Clark, because she was the wife of an important American industrialist. She was found strangled in the staff changing room of the Hotel Majestic. Interest focuses first of all on an employee of the hotel, Donge, and his mistress Charlotte. But the next day there is another murder: that of the hotel porter. Against Maigret's advice the examining magistrate has the couple arrested. Maigret then discovers that the American woman had formerly been the mistress of Donge, and that there is a child from that relationship. Someone had been blackmailing Mrs. Clark, imitating Donge's handwriting, and her arrival in Paris threatened to unmask the criminal.

Comments: The daily life of a big hotel is very convincingly conveyed, especially from the perspective of those who work there. Maigret soaks up the atmosphere and discovers the murderer through his intuitive grasp of psychology. 5/5

22) Maigret In Exile

(*La maison du juge*, in *Maigret Revient*, 1942). Hamilton, 1978; Harcourt, USA, 1979; Harvest 136, USA, 1979; and in the volume of three novels under the same title, *Maigret In Exile* (Penguin 5160, 1983).

Plot: Maigret is a superintendent at Lucon and goes to solve a crime at L'Aiguillon. A retired judge discovers the body of an unknown man in his house. The judge has a son, Albert, and a daughter, Lise. He lives with his daughter, who is a little retarded and willingly sleeps with the young men in the village. One of these men, Marcel Airaud, disappears as soon as Maigret arrives. The judge eventually confesses to Maigret that fifteen years before he murdered his wife's lover. The judge is arrested and Maigret discovers that the man found dead in the judge's house was a psychiatrist. The situation appears even more complex when it is revealed that Lise is pregnant. All these facts are woven neatly together in the conclusion, though in a rather complex way.

Comments: Maigret sets out to solve one crime and solves another by chance. Some may find the twists and turns of the plot difficult to follow at times. 3/5

23) To Any Lengths

(*Signé Picpus*, in a volume of three short Maigret novels and five other short stories under the title *Signé Picpus*, 1944). Routledge, 1950; Penguin 1225, 1958.

Plot: A frightened bank clerk comes to Maigret with a piece of blotting paper, which he has found in a restaurant. On it the following words are written back to front: 'Tomorrow afternoon on the stroke of five I am going to kill the fortune-teller.' The police wait for possible bad news and wonder if it is all a hoax. Confirmation arrives. When Maigret arrives on the scene he finds not only the dead fortune-teller but also a poor old man waiting patiently. He does not believe that the old man is the culprit, however. But Maigret does discover that the man changed his identity to help a widow get round the law. Then someone discovered what he was up to.

Comments: The novel is especially noteworthy for its confrontation between Maigret and the examining magistrate. 3/5

24) Maigret's Rival

(*L'Inspecteur Cadavre*, in a volume of three short Maigret novels and five other short stories under the title *Signé Picpus*, 1944). Hamilton, 1979; Harcourt, USA, 1980; Harvest 148, USA, 1985; and in a volume of three novels under the title *Maigret's Rival* (Penguin 5468, 1985).

Plot: A man is run over by a train in a small town in the Vendée. A rich property owner, Naud, whose father-in-law is a judge in Paris asks Maigret to investigate the affair, because the rumour is spreading that he caused the man's death. Maigret encounters a private detective called Cavre, who is a former detective from his own department, and nicknamed 'Inspector Corpse' (because of the similarity between his real name 'Cavre' and the French word for corpse, 'cadavre'). As ever Maigret is not happy investigating the lives of people in high society. It turns out that the murdered man has seduced a young girl, who is pregnant by another man. And there has been a general attempt to cover up the whole business. Maigret is sickened by the facts he uncovers and returns to Paris without making an arrest.

Comments: Another example of Maigret passing judgement himself and letting the culprit go free. He realizes that there is insufficient evidence to convict and that bringing it to court would just stir up a lot of dirt. 3/5

25) Maigret And The Toy Village

(*Felicie est là*, in a volume of three short Maigret novels and five short stories under the title *Signé Picpus*, 1944). Hamilton, 1978; Harcourt, USA, 1979; in a volume of three novels under the title *Maigret In Exile* (Penguin 5160, 1983); and Harvest 154, 1987.

Plot: Maigret goes to investigate the murder of a retired accountant living in the Jeannville Estate, a few miles from Paris. He was shot in his own bedroom at point-blank range. It is a pretty ideal little world, which seems unreal to Maigret, like a toy village in fact. He becomes fascinated by the character and behaviour of the old man's servant, Félicie, who is in love with the victim's nephew, Jacques. This young man is badly wounded in the Place Pigalle, but refuses to explain the circumstances. Félicie fears that he may be the murderer, but Maigret discovers that it has more to do with the suspicious company he has been keeping. Jacques knows too much about someone's past criminal activities.

Comments: This is a charming and unusual novel with the main focus on the complex personality of Félicie, who lies, contradicts herself, indulges in bizarre flights of the imagination and craves sympathy and understanding. 5/5

26) Death Of A Nobody

Short Story. ('On ne tue pas les pauvres types', in the collection of short stories *Maigret et L'Inspecteur Malchanceux*, 1947). See: 30) *Maigret And The Surly Inspector* and 39) *Maigret's Christmas*.

Plot: A quiet and self-effacing man is killed in his own home. There seems no obvious reason for killing such a poor man. But Maigret discovers that he has been leading a double life.

Comments: Leading a double life is a theme which recurs again and again in Simenon's works, and notably in the best of the 'romans durs'. 3/5

27) Maigret In Retirement

Short Story. ('Maigret se fâche', published together with 'La Pipe de Maigret', 1947). Published together with other short stories in *Maigret's Christmas* (Hamilton, 1976; Harcourt, USA, 1977; Harvest 132, USA, 1981; Penguin 4931, 1981).

Plot: While in retirement Maigret is asked by Bernadette Amorelle to investigate the suspicious circumstances surrounding the drowning of her granddaughter, Monita. He goes to Paris and along the Seine to investigate the girl's wealthy family background. He meets Bernadette's son-in-law, Ernest Malik, who turns out to have been to the same school as Maigret. Eventually he discovers that Monita was provoked into suicide by the revelation that she was in love with her own half-brother. This leads to a further death, from anger and a desire for revenge. All kinds of family secrets come to light, including adultery and the obsession with money.

Comments: Maigret finally manages to establish some kind of order in this family torn apart by passion and resentment, who have nevertheless struggled to maintain an appearance of respectability (a theme that recurs frequently in many of Simenon's 'romans durs'). 3/5

28) Maigret's Pipe

Short Story. ('La Pipe de Maigret', published together with 'Maigret se fâche', 1947). Published together with other short stories under the title *Maigret's Pipe* (Hamilton, 1977; Harcourt, USA, 1978; Penguin 4930, 1984; Harvest 146, USA, 1985).

Plot: Madame Leroy seeks Maigret's help when she discovers that someone is searching her house when she is away. The following night her son Joseph disappears at the very same time as Maigret's pipe! Maigret discovers that Joseph has links with a crook who is looking for something in the house.

Comments: This short story is not without humour. Needless to say, Maigret solves the crime…and gets back his pipe!

Note: The other short stories featuring Maigret in the English editions have complex individual publication histories, which are not worth tracing here. They were all originally published together in French, without 'La Pipe de Maigret', in *Les Nouvelles Enquêtes de Maigret*, 1944. Most of them were written in1936 and 1938. They did not appear together in English until their publication in the collection *Maigret's Pipe*, without the story 'Jeumont, 51 Minutes Wait!' in the Harcourt and Harvest editions. The stories are: 'Death Penalty'('Peine de mort'); 'Mr. Monday' ('Monsieur Lundi'); Jeumont, 51 Minutes Wait!' ('Jeumont, 51 minutes d'arrêt'); 'The Open Window' ('La fenêtre ouverte'); 'Madame Maigret's Admirer' ('L'amoureux de Madame Maigret'); 'The Mysterious Affair In The Boulevard Beaumarchais' ('L'affaire du boulevard Beaumarchais'); 'Two Bodies On A Barge' ('La péniche aux deux pendus'); 'Death Of A Woodlander' ('Les larmes de bougie'); 'In The Rue Pigalle' ('Rue Pigalle'); 'Maigret's Mistake' ('Un erreur de Maigret'); 'The Old Lady Of Bayeux' ('La vieille dame de Bayeux'); 'Stan The Killer' ('Stan le tueur'); 'The Drowned Men's Inn' ('L'Auberge aux Noyés'); 'At the Etoile Du Nord' ('L'Etoile du Nord'); 'Mademoiselle Berthe And Her Lover' ('Mademoiselle Berthe et son amant'); 'The Three Daughters Of The Lawyer' ('Le notaire de Châteauneuf'); 'Storm In The Channel' ('Tempête sur la Manche'). 3/5

29) Maigret In New York's Underworld

(*Maigret à New York*, 1947). Doubleday, USA, 1955. Translated as *Inspector Maigret In New York's Underworld* (Signet 1338, 1956) and as *Maigret In New York* (Hamilton, 1979). Also included as *Maigret In New York* in a volume of three novels under the title *Maigret's Rival* (Penguin 5468, 1985).

Plot: While Maigret is enjoying his retirement on the banks of the Loire, he is contacted by a young man who is worried about his father, Joachim Maura, known as John, a New York businessman, who seems to be in some distress according to his letters. Maigret agrees to go with the young man to New York to investigate. There, with the help of his friend, Captain O'Brien, of the FBI he discovers some unsavoury facts about Joachim Maura's background. Some gangsters know these facts too and are blackmailing him. Maigret manages to get the gangsters arrested but he remains uneasy about his role in the whole affair.

Comments: Many aficionados are not happy with this venture of Maigret beyond his usual territory. And Maigret himself does not seem to have enjoyed his trip very much. At the end he is thinking more about the need to thin out his melon plants in the hotbeds back home in Meung-sur-Loire. 2/5

30) Maigret And The Surly Inspector

Short Story. ('Maigret et l'inspecteur malchanceux', published in the collection of short stories *Maigret et l'inspecteur malchanceux*, 1947. Later the title of both story and collection was changed to *Maigret et l'inspecteur Malgracieux*). Included in the collection of short stories called *Maigret's Christmas* (Hamilton, 1976; Harcourt, USA, 1977; Harvest, USA, 1981; Penguin 4931, 1981).

Plot: A message comes through on a public emergency telephone. Someone shouts 'Merde to the cops!' and then there is a shot. A body is subsequently discovered near the Rue Caulaincourt. When Maigret arrives on the scene he is handed the dead man's wallet, which reveals that the victim is a thirty-eight-year-old diamond broker. Inspector Lognon hopes the case might help him to make his mark, but Maigret is always hovering in the background. When the mystery is unraveled as an insurance fraud at the end, Maigret does his best to give Lognon the credit and invites him to dinner. But Lognon remains surly to the last.

Comment: The story is memorable for the introduction of Inspector Lognon, who appears also in six Maigret novels. He is nicknamed 'malchanceux' (unlucky) because he never seems to get any good cases which would help him to gain promotion. His colleagues also describe him as 'malgracieux' (clumsy, or ungainly) because of his dour and sombre manner. 3/5

Note: This short story was included together with three others in the original French edition: 'The Evidence Of The Altar-boy' ('Le témoinage de l'enfant de choeur'); 'The Most Obstinate Customer In The World' ('Le client le plus obstiné du monde'); and 'Death Of A Nobody' ('On ne tue pas les pauvres gens'). See also 26) 'Death Of A Nobody'. Their English translations have complex individual publication histories. They were first published altogether in English with five other Maigret stories in the volume entitled *Maigret's Christmas*. See 39) *Maigret's Christmas* for fuller details.

31) Maigret's Special Murder

(*Maigret et son mort*, 1948). Hamilton, 1964; Penguin 2471, 1966; in *A Maigret Quartet* (Hamilton, 1972); and translated as *Maigret's Dead Man* (Doubleday, USA, 1964).

Plot: An unknown man feels that his life is in danger and seeks the protection of the police, but Inspector Janvier cannot find him again. The following night the man is murdered. Maigret takes the case personally, regarding it as his murder. In the course of his investigations he pursues a yellow Citroën, which leads him to the café in Charenton, of which the dead man, Albert, was the landlord. One suspect is chased by the police but is killed by his fellow crooks. Maigret is however able to identify the dead suspect and get on the trail of the so-called 'Picardy Killers'. Albert, it seems, knew more than was good for him.

Comments: Maigret comes across in this novel very much as a man of action. Some have criticized the evocations of Parisian locations as rather sketchy. 2/5

32) A Summer Holiday

(*Les vacances de Maigret*, 1948). Included with another novel in *Maigret On Holiday* (Routledge Kegan Paul, 1950). Translated as *No Vacation For Maigret* (Doubleday, USA, 1953; Bantam 1875, 1959). Newly translated as *Maigret on Holiday* (Penguin 2898, 1970).

Plot: While Maigret and his wife are on holiday in Les Sables-d'Olonne, Mme Maigret has to go into a convent nursing home for an operation on her appendix. While she is there a fellow patient, a certain Hélène Godreau dies of a suspected skull fracture. Maigret's curiosity is aroused and he gets to know the brother-in-law of the victim, Dr. Bellamy, who is known to be a jealous husband. The following night a young girl called Lucile is murdered and her brother Emile disappears mysteriously. It appears that the doctor's wife and Emile have been having an affair. Linking the crimes is a web of passions and jealousies.

Comments: It is a neatly tied-up mystery, with Maigret conducting his investigations unofficially. The character of the doctor is very well realized. 4/5

33) Maigret's First Case

(*La première enquête de Maigret*, 1949). Hamilton,1956; Penguin 1594, 1961; in *The Second Maigret Omnibus*, (Hamilton, 1964); in *Maigret Cinq*, Harcourt, USA, 1965; Heinemann Educational, 1970.

Plot: The story is set in 1913 when Maigret was still secretary to a superintendent in a small Paris police station. A young flautist informs the police that he has heard gunfire in a large town-house, but when Maigret accompanies him there they can find no evidence of anything unusual having happened. But the behaviour of the owners, the family called Gendreau-Balthazar, seems suspicious to Maigret, and he carries out a discreet investigation. He discovers that the comte d'Anseval was murdered because he refused to marry Lise Gendreau-Balthazar. There is a cover up and an attempt to make the crime look like self-defence.

Comments: It may have been the first time in his career but it certainly was not to be the last time that Maigret was disgusted at the behaviour of the upper classes of society. Not a typical Maigret investigation, but the future chief inspector already reveals his talent for psychological intuition. The novel ends with Maigret being appointed inspector. It also provides insights into the life of the newlywed Maigrets. 3/5

34) My Friend Maigret

(*Mon ami Maigret*, 1949). Hamilton, 1956; Penguin 1419, 1959; in *Maigret Triumphant*, (Hamilton, 1969). Translated as *The Methods Of Maigret*, (Doubleday, USA, 1957; Bantam A2063, 1959).

Plot: Maigret is being visited by Inspector Pyke of Scotland Yard, who has come over to study French methods of detection. His routine is disturbed by a telephone call from the Mediterranean island of Porquerolles. An old tramp, called Marcellin, has been murdered there, and the night before he was heard talking to people about his 'friend Maigret'. Maigret is glad to get away from Paris for a while, though the prospect of taking Inspector Pyke with him does not please him. They discover that a blackmail racket is behind the murder.

Comments: The situation of a small island with only a limited number of suspects may be a cliché of crime fiction, but Simenon makes the seaside atmosphere, with its small square and café, irresistible. Maigret is obviously ill at ease throughout in the presence of Inspector Pyke, but the juxtaposition of the two characters serves to highlight the differences in their methods: the plodding logic of the Englishman and the unconventional intuitive methods of the Frenchman. 4/5

35) Maigret And The Coroner

(*Maigret chez le coroner*, 1949). Hamilton, 1980. Translated as *Maigret At The Coroner's* (Harcourt, USA, 1980; Harvest 143, 1984).

Plot: Maigret has been invited by the FBI to observe an investigation in the USA. A woman called Bessy has been murdered near Tucson, and five young airmen are being interrogated by the coroner. After interviewing several witnesses it is discovered that the young woman had gone out with all five of the airmen and was mortally wounded while trying to resist the advances of one of them, who was determined to have his way with her.

Comments: Maigret is only present as an observer and even has to leave before the jury reaches its decision. Many readers have therefore found the outcome rather disappointing. The novel does however provide interesting insights into the way the American system of justice is organized. 2/5

36) Maigret And The Old Lady

(*Maigret et la vieille dame*, 1950). Hamilton, 1958; Penguin 1678, 1962; in *The Second Maigret Omnibus* (Hamilton, 1964); in *Maigret Cinq* (Harcourt, 1965).

Plot: Valentine Besson, an old lady, tells Maigret of her belief that the poison that killed her servant, Rose, was really intended for her. Suspicion falls on the old woman's children, but then another death occurs. The old lady kills Rose's brother, whom she apparently mistakes for a prowler. All is not quite what it seems in the old lady's family.

Comments: Perhaps a rather contrived plot, but the character of the old lady is very convincingly realized. 4/5

37) Madame Maigret's Own Case

(*L'amie de Madame Maigret*, 1950). Doubleday, USA, 1959. Translated as *Madame Maigret's Friend* (Hamilton, 1960; Penguin 2571, 1967), which was also included in *Maigret: A Fifth Omnibus* (Hamilton, 1973).

Plot: The police arrest a Belgian bookbinder called Steuvels, following the appearance of some anonymous letters. They find blood and human remains in his house. But Steuvels denies everything, and the investigation makes no headway. When Maigret's wife comments on the strange behaviour of a young woman whom she often meets in a public garden, he is able to spot a link between two cases. The young woman is involved with a gang who killed a rich Italian widow, whose son-in-law is also an accomplice of the gang. It turns out that Steuvels also has links with the gang.

Comments: The connections between two cases are intriguingly developed. And the novel is memorable for the important role of Madame Maigret. 5/5

38) Maigret's Memoirs

(*Les mémoires de Maigret*, 1951). Hamilton, 1963; Penguin 2503, 1966; Harcourt, USA, 1985; also included in *Maigret Victorious* (Hamilton, 1975).

Plot: Having settled into retirement Maigret decides to write his memoirs and compare his own memories with the portrait of him provided by a certain novelist called Georges Simenon. There is no plot as such, no mystery and its investigation. The reader is simply provided with reflections on various stages of Maigret's life, filling in a few gaps here and there in what the reader has been able to learn from reading the novels. Maigret takes issue with some of Simenon's opinions and depictions of him and adds a few thoughts on the life of a policeman and the nature of justice. It is also a book about writing, about distinctions between art and reality: a fictional character talks about himself as though he were real, and the real author is introduced as a character in this fiction.

Comments: A charming book, utterly different from all the other Maigrets, but can only be of interest to those who have read a large number of the Maigret novels before coming to it. 3/5

39) Maigret's Christmas

Short Story. ('Un noël de Maigret', included with two other short stories in *Un noël de Maigret*, 1951). In *The Short Cases of Inspector Maigret* (Doubleday, 1959). Together with eight other stories in *Maigret's Christmas* (Hamilton, 1976; Harcourt, USA, 1977; Penguin 4931, 1981; Harvest 132, 1981).

Plot: A young girl, Colette Martin, living near the Maigrets, tells her neighbour that she saw Santa Claus in her room on Christmas Eve. Her Aunt Loraine follows the neighbour's suggestion and asks Maigret's advice. He discovers that the 'Santa Claus' in question was in fact a murderer with an ulterior motive. And Aunt Loraine proves not to be as innocent as she may look.

Comment: An intriguing tale set in and around Maigret's apartment. 4/5

Note: The volume *Maigret's Christmas* contains this story and eight others. One of them, 'Seven Little Crosses In A Notebook' ('Sept petites croix dans un carnet'), is not a Maigret story, though it is set in police headquarters, and he is conspicuous by his absence. The others are 'Maigret And The Surly Inspector' ('Maigret et l'inspecteur malgracieux'), for which see also 30) 'Maigret And The Surly Inspector' above; 'The Evidence Of The Altar-Boy' ('Le témoinage de l'enfant de choeur'); 'The Most Obstinate Customer In The World' ('Le client le plus obstiné du monde'); 'Sale By Auction' ('Vente à bougie'); 'The Man In The Street' ('L'homme dans la rue'); 'Maigret In Retirement' ('Maigret se fâche'). Their English translations have complex individual publication histories, which are not worth tracing here.

40) Maigret In Montmartre

(*Maigret au 'Picratt's'*, 1951). In *Maigret Right And Wrong* (Hamilton, 1954). Translated as *Inspector Maigret And The Strangled Stripper* (Double-day, 1954). Translated as *Maigret In Montmartre* (Penguin 1221, 1958; in *A Maigret Omnibus*, Hamilton, 1962; and in *Five Times Maigret*, Harcourt, USA, 1964).

Plot: The action centers round a small nightclub called 'Picratt's' in Mont-martre. A striptease artist called Arlette informs the police that she has over-heard two men planning to murder someone they refer to as 'the countess', and the name Oscar was mentioned. The police do not really believe there is any-thing in her story, but shortly after she herself is found murdered. Working together again with the lugubrious Inspector Lognon, Maigret now takes Arlette's story seriously. Sure enough it is not long before a countess is found murdered. And a crook called Oscar does seem to have an important role in the affair.

Comments: Most critics and fans agree in their appreciation of this novel, with its vivid evocation of Montmartre. 5/5

41) Maigret Takes A Room

(*Maigret en meublé*, 1951). Hamilton, 1960; in *The Second Maigret Omni-bus*, Hamilton, 1964; Penguin 2249, 1965; in *Maigret Cinq*, Harcourt, USA, 1965. Also translated as *Maigret Rents A Room*, Doubleday, USA, 1961.

Plot: After a robbery a young delinquent called Emile disappears. Then Inspector Janvier is badly wounded while watching the young man's lodgings in the Rue Lhomond. But it does not seem likely that a young man who had robbed a till with a toy pistol would shoot a policeman with a real gun. As Madame Maigret is away in Alsace visiting her sister who is due to have an operation, Maigret decides to take a room in the same building so that he can watch and question everybody. The young man is eventually found staying with his landlord. It turns out that someone misunderstood why Janvier was watching the house.

Comments: Simenon is a master at evoking the life of Parisian lodging houses, and this is a prime example. Maigret arrests the would-be murderer rather reluctantly after hearing the full story. 5/5

42) Maigret And The Burglar's Wife

(*Maigret et la grande perche*, 1951). Hamilton, 1955; Penguin 1362, 1959; and in *Maigret Triumphant*, Hamilton, 1989. Also translated as *Inspector Mai-gret And The Burglar's Wife* (Doubleday, USA, 1956).

Plot: A former prostitute whom Maigret had arrested in the past comes to see him because she is worried about her husband. She goes by the nickname of Lofty (in J. Maclaren-Ross' English translation). In French 'la grande perche' is roughly equivalent to 'Beanpole'. Seventeen years before, when Maigret was an inexperienced policeman, she had removed all her clothes in an attempt to prevent him taking her to the police station. Now her husband, Alfred (known as 'Sad Freddie'), who is a rather unlucky burglar specializing in safe breaking, has had a rather unfortunate experience while breaking into a house: he came across the blood-soaked body of a woman. He has therefore decided to go into hiding rather than get involved in a murder enquiry. According to Lofty the house belonged to a wealthy dentist living near the Bois de Boulogne. Maigret visits the dentist, Guillaume Serre, who has been living with his mother and his wife, who seems to have decided to leave him the very night of the attempted burglary. Finally a whole string of murders is traced.

Comments: A particularly fascinating mystery, with Maigret pitted against a clever opponent. 5/5

43) Inspector Maigret And The Killers

(*Maigret, Lognon at les gangsters*, 1952). Doubleday, USA, 1954. Translated as *Maigret And The Gangsters* (Hamilton, 1974; in *The Twelfth Simenon Omnibus*, Penguin 4431, 1977; Harcourt, USA, 1986).

Plot: Inspector Lognon is as unlucky as ever. He still seems unable to make any advancement in his career. One night he witnesses an attack and perhaps a murder. It seems to be the chance he has been waiting for. He decides to act alone against some formidable American gangsters. But Maigret is called in and undertakes the investigation with the help of Lognon and the FBI. Two of the gang are caught and arrested and there is news of another murder, probably by the same gang, in the USA.

Comments: For once Lognon proves his worth. Without his dogged persistence the police would not have known about the two murderers. Maigret is hurt and annoyed by the disrespectful attitude of the American police, which spurs him even more to wind up the case. 3/5

44) Maigret's Revolver

(*Le revolver de Maigret*, 1952). Hamilton, 1979; Penguin 1363, 1959; Harcourt, USA, 1984; Harvest 141, USA, 1984. Also with two other novels in *Maigret's Rival* (Penguin 5468, 1985).

Plot: A young man wants to discuss something with Maigret at his home, but finding that he is not there, manages to steal his revolver. Shortly after this incident Maigret encounters a man called Lagrange, who is worried about the fact that his son has disappeared, and he realizes that there is a link between the two incidents. It turns out that Lagrange is in fact a blackmailer who has also become a killer. Maigret manages to prevent a final tragedy, but it turns out to be difficult to prove the guilt of the person who is really behind it all.

Comments: One aspect of this novel that makes it unique is that part of it takes place in London, where he is helped by an old acquaintance, Inspector

Pyke of Scotland Yard. In the course of his investigation Maigret develops an almost fatherly affection for the young thief he is pursuing. 4/5

45) Maigret And The Man On The Boulevard

(*Maigret et l'homme du banc*, 1953). Hamilton, 1975. Translated also as *Maigret And The Man On The Bench* (Harcourt, 1975; Harvest 123, USA, 1979; and in *The Thirteenth Simenon Omnibus*, Penguin 4511, 1978).

Plot: Louis Thouret is murdered in a cul-de-sac in Paris. There is no apparent motive for the crime. The man's wife proves to be contemptuous of her husband, and while she can readily identify the body, she admits to being puzzled by the fact that he was wearing light brown shoes and a garish tie she had never seen before. Maigret discovers that Thouret only pretended to go to work everyday and had in fact been made redundant three years before. He had been surviving by committing burglaries.

Comments: This novel provides a fascinating treatment of a common Simenon theme: the attempt to escape from failure and a dull uninteresting life. In this case the attempt fails. 4/5

46) Maigret Afraid

(*Maigret a peur*, 1953). Hamilton, 1961; Penguin 2250, 1965; Harcourt, USA, 1983; Harvest 142, USA, 1984; and in *Maigret Triumphant* (Hamilton, 1969).

Plot: Maigret is returning from an international police conference and decides to take a detour to visit an old friend, the magistrate Chabot, in the country town of Fontenay-le-Comte. His friend is mystified by a series of murders, which have all been committed using the same weapon but against victims who appear to have been chosen randomly. One was an old aristocrat, another a midwife and one was an old drunkard. Although he is not actually in charge of the case, Maigret helps the local police. The local police are baffled by the case, but Maigret is intrigued by it, especially when he discovers that one of the victims was the brother-in-law of a certain Hubert Vernoux de Courçon. He fears there may be further murders, including his own.

Comments: Some have found this novel disappointing because Maigret remains somewhat aloof from events, but there are many subtle Simenon characterizations to enjoy. 3/5

47) Maigret's Mistake

(*Maigret se trompe*, 1953). In *Maigret Right And Wrong* (Hamilton, 1954); Penguin 1222, 1958; in *A Maigret Omnibus* (Hamilton, 1962); in *Five Times Maigret* (Harcourt, USA, 1964).

Plot: A former prostitute, Louise Filon, is murdered in the sumptuous apartment that she has been living in for the past two years. There are no obvious clues at first so Maigret investigates the lives of her clients. Two men in particular interest him, her lover and the man who has been supporting her financially. Both of these are prime suspects because it is discovered that Louise was pregnant. The final resolution to the mystery is brought about by a confession.

Comments: Maigret conducts an admirably rigorous investigation, and there is an interesting contrast in the social backgrounds of the two suspects. 5/5

48) Maigret Goes to School

(*Maigret à l'école*, 1954). Hamilton, 1957; Four Square 191, 1960; in *A Maigret Omnibus* (Hamilton, 1962); in *Five Times Maigret* (Harcourt, USA, 1964); Longman, 1974; Penguin 6919, 1992.

Plot: The novel takes place in the small village of Saint-André, near La Rochelle. Gastin, the schoolteacher, is accused by the local police of killing the old postmistress, Léonie Birard, by shooting her. Everyone despised her because she was especially spiteful and malicious, taunting the children and slandering their parents. Gastin begs Maigret to prove his innocence by finding the real killer. Taking a sort of working holiday, Maigret moves into the small village. The victim lived quite close to the school, which was why Gastin is an obvious suspect, although he claims he was not there at the time. Maigret solves the mystery by befriending one of the local children.

Comments: Maigret defies public opinion in the village and follows his usual intuitive methods. The novel is memorable for the subtle relationship between Maigret and a local schoolboy, whom he interrogates with great sensitivity. 5/5

49) Maigret And The Young Girl

(*Maigret et la jeune morte*, 1954). Hamilton, 1955; in *The Second Maigret Omnibus* (Hamilton, 1964); in *Maigret Cinq* (Harcourt, USA, 1965); also translated as *Inspector Maigret And The Dead Girl* (Doubleday, USA, 1955).

Plot: A young girl is murdered in Inspector Lognon's sector, but as usual for the hapless inspector, Maigret takes over as it appears to be a complicated case. After conducting a very long investigation Maigret discovers that the girl died following a series of unfortunate circumstances. She had received a letter informing her that she would inherit a large fortune from her father, a criminal who was dying. But the letter was intercepted.

Comments: As usual when Lognon is present, Maigret's methods are shown to be very effective by contrast. Lognon plods on in a routine way, while Maigret discovers the truth by understanding the victim's personality. 3/5

50) Maigret And The Minister

(*Maigret chez le ministre*, 1955). Hamilton, 1969; in *The Third Simenon Omnibus* (Penguin 3324, 1971); also translated as *Maigret And The Calamé Report* (Harcourt, USA, 1969; Harvest 153, USA, 1987).

Plot: Maigret is asked by a minister to conduct a discreet enquiry to find a report, the Calamé report, which has gone missing. The material would be political dynamite if it got into the wrong hands because it proves government responsibility for a major disaster. However the press somehow learns of it, probably from the person who stole it, and the minister finds himself in an embarrassing situation. It appears that another unscrupulous politician is behind it all.

Comments: Maigret does not prove to be very successful in this case, revealing thereby his basic humanity, but the novel provides a devastating condemnation of the duplicity of political life. 4/5

51) Maigret And The Headless Corpse

(*Maigret et le corps sans tête*, 1955). Hamilton, 1967; Harcourt, USA, 1968; in *The Fourth Simenon Omnibus* (Penguin 3337, 1971); in *Maigret Victorious* (Hamilton, 1975); Harvest 144, USA, 1985.

Plot: Various parts of a man's body are fished out of the Saint-Martin canal in Paris after it has fouled the propeller of a barge, but the head is missing. Maigret pursues his investigations in the area around a small bistro frequented by seamen and dockers on the quayside at Valmy. The owner of the bistro has gone missing. The headless corpse is finally identified by a scar. It proves to be the owner of the bistro, Omer Callas, and suspicion focuses on his wife and her lover, who had had a violent argument with Callas concerning an inheritance.

Comments: The crime in this novel is almost incidental to the intriguing study of relationships. 4/5

52) Maigret Sets a Trap

(*Maigret tend un piège*, 1955). Hamilton, 1965; Penguin 2796, 1968; Harcourt, USA, 1972; Harvest 126, USA, 1979.

Plot: Five women have been horribly murdered in the streets of Montmartre. Feeling angry and weary Maigret decides to set a trap to try and catch the killer. A huge police operation is conducted but somehow the criminal manages to escape. However, a young policewoman in plain clothes who acts as bait manages to grab a button from the attacker's coat. A young man called Marcel Moncin is arrested, but then a sixth crime is committed.

Comments: The real strength of this novel is in the profound study of the psychology of the murderer, utterly convincing, and reminiscent of some of the best 'romans durs'. 5/5

53) Maigret's Failure

(*Un échec de Maigret*, 1956). Hamilton, 1962; Penguin 2248, 1965; in *A Maigret Quartet* (Hamilton, 1972); in *A Maigret Trio* (Harcourt, USA, 1973; Harvest 137, USA, 1983).

Plot: An old acquaintance of Maigret's, an industrialist named Ferdinand Fumal, asks for protection after receiving anonymous letters. Despite the fact that Maigret has him watched, he is found dead the next day. In the course of his investigations Maigret discovers that the man was detested by his staff and despised by his family. There appear to be an enormous number of suspects, and the investigation makes slow progress. Maigret unravels the mystery rather belatedly.

Comments: The delay in Maigret's solving of the mystery is undoubtedly due to his lack of concern about the victim, whom he disliked. 3/5

54) Maigret's Little Joke

(*Maigret s'amuse*, 1957). Hamilton, 1957; in *The Second Maigret Omnibus* (Hamilton, 1964); in *Maigret Cinq* (Harcourt, USA, 1965); also translated as *None Of Maigret's Business* (Doubleday, USA, 1958; Bantam, 1960).

Plot: While taking a holiday on doctor's orders, but staying in Paris, Maigret is intrigued by an investigation being conducted by one of his inspectors, Janvier. It concerns the suspicious death of Evelyne, wife of a certain Dr. Jave. She should have been on the Côte d'Azur and not in Paris at all. Maigret does not want to interfere directly in Janvier's case, so he sends him anonymous messages; these provide some help and eventually enable him to discover how she was murdered and who did it.

Comments: Maigret follows the case at a distance, and gathers his information by reading newspapers, taking a few walks in Paris and making a few anonymous phone calls. He obviously enjoys conducting an investigation in this playful way for a change. 4/5

55) Maigret And The Millionaires

(*Maigret voyage*, 1958). Hamilton, 1974; Harcourt, USA, 1974; in *The Eleventh Simenon Omnibus* (Penguin 4248, 1977); Harvest 150, USA, 1986.

Plot: Colonel Ward is found drowned in his bath in a luxury suite in the Hôtel George V, and his mistress, the Countess Paverini, attempted suicide the previous night. Maigret makes enquiries about the countess' second husband, Joseph Van Meulen, a Belgian industrialist, and investigates the shady past of the countess. The colonel's third wife also comes under suspicion.

Comments: As usual Maigret feels ill at ease in the world of high society, but persists in employing his usual investigative methods. 4/5

56) Maigret Has Scruples

(*Les scrupules de Maigret*, 1958). Hamilton, 1959; in *Versus Inspector Maigret* (Doubleday, USA, 1960); Penguin 1680, 1962; in *A Maigret Omnibus* (Hamilton, 1962); in *Five Times Maigret* (Harcourt, USA, 1964).

Plot: Xavier Marton, a salesman of toy electric trains in a large store, believes his wife Gisèle is planning to murder him because he has found zinc phosphide in the broom cupboard. After being contacted by Marton, Maigret is also approached by his wife. Maigret's investigation implicates two other people: Marton's sister-in-law Jenny and an acquaintance of Gisèle, who is also her lover. Soon Marton is found poisoned. It turns out however that a fatal error has occurred.

Comments: It has been felt by many that this novel concerns itself more with psychological investigation than with questions of justice, but this could be said of many of Simenon's works. 3/5

57) Maigret And The Reluctant Witnesses

(*Maigret et les témoins récalcitrants*, 1959). In *Versus Inspector Maigret* (Doubleday, USA, 1960); Hamilton, 1959; Penguin 1681, 1962; in *A Maigret Omnibus* (Hamilton, 1962); in *Five Times Maigret* (Harcourt, USA, 1964).

Plot: An industrialist called Lachaume has been murdered in bed at his home in Ivry. The family owns a company making petits-beurre biscuits, which were once a household name. The family lawyer is immediately called in and it is agreed to put up a wall of silence against all investigation. Maigret, however, will not be put off and eventually rules out the theory of burglary, believing that the culprit is to be found in Lachaume's immediate entourage. The focus narrows when it is discovered that the family business is on the verge of bankruptcy.

Comments: Maigret is not in a good mood during this case, for various reasons: his wife has just reminded him that he will be retiring in two years; his old office stove has been taken away; the new examining magistrate, Angelot, is breathing down his neck; and the Lachaumes are defensive and refuse to talk. It requires a great deal of his famed patience to discover the culprit. 4/5

58) Maigret Has Doubts

(*Une confidence de Maigret*, 1959). Hamilton, 1968; in *The Third Simenon Omnibus*, Penguin 3324, 1971; Harcourt, USA, 1982.

Plot: A manufacturer of pharmaceutical products, Adriann Josset, is suspected of having killed his wife Christine. The couple did not get on very well, and Josset had a mistress. Despite the evidence against him, Maigret is convinced that he is innocent, but he cannot find the real murderer, and only learns who it is too late.

Comments: Confiding in his friend Dr. Pardon this time proves to be a mistake for Maigret. The novel can be read as a firm statement against capital punishment. 3/5

59) Maigret In Court

(*Maigret aux assises*, 1960). Hamilton, 1961; Penguin 2251, 1965; in *Maigret Triumphant* (Hamilton, 1969; Harcourt, USA, 1983.

Plot: Maigret has to give an account in the assize court on an investigation conducted several months previously, concerning the murder of Léontine Faverges and Cécile, the young girl who lives with her. Certain clues and an anonymous accusation seem to indicate that Léontine's nephew, Gaston Meurant is responsible, but he is acquitted due to a lack of sufficient evidence. Maigret decides to pursue the investigation further and considers the role of Ginette, who married Meurant, and has a background in the world of cabaret, and that of her present lover. The end of the novel has a rather ironical twist.

Comments: Apart from the fascination of the story itself, the novel is interesting for its reflection of the processes of justice and their limitations. 3/5

60) Maigret In Society

(*Maigret et les vieillards*, 1960). Hamilton, 1962; Penguin 2247, 1965; in *A Maigret Quartet* (Hamilton, 1962); in *A Maigret Trio* (Harcourt, USA, 1973; Harvest, USA, 1983).

Plot: The old Comte Armand de Saint-Hilaire is found dead, shot many times over, in the study of his home near the Boulevard Saint-Germain. Maigret discovers that there had been a platonic relationship between the old count and Princess Isabelle, who has been recently widowed. They had planned to marry when she became free. In the meantime they had written to each other and observed each other occasionally from a distance. It is a world in which Maigret does not feel at ease. There seem to be no obvious suspects in the case, and the surly old housekeeper does not exactly help Maigret in his enquiries. When the truth finally comes to light it is moving and sad.

Comments: Maigret feels considerable relief when this case is over. Such a rarified concept of love seems almost unreal to him. It is worth noting that Simenon wrote of this novel in his collection of notes entitled *When I Was Old (Quand j'étais vieux*, 1960*)*: 'Now I think it's the best of the Maigrets.' 5/5

61) Maigret And The Lazy Burglar

(*Maigret et le voleur paresseux*, 1961). Hamilton, 1963; Penguin 2526, 1967; in *A Maigret Quartet* (Hamilton, 1972); in *A Maigret Trio* (Harcourt, USA, 1973; Harvest, USA, 1983).

Plot: A burglar, Cuendet, is found dead in the Bois de Boulogne. The magistrates do not consider it an urgent case. Maigret, who is called in by another inspector, decides to focus on the personality of Cuendet. He discovers that the burglar had commited a final crime just before his death. For embarrassing personal reasons a cover-up became necessary.

Comments: Even though Maigret eventually discovers the truth, he fails to convince the examining magistrate, despite the existence of material evidence. Throughout the whole novel there is a sense of confrontation between the police and the system of justice. 4/5

62) Maigret And The Black Sheep

(*Maigret et les braves gens*, 1962). Hamilton, 1976; Harcourt, USA, 1976; in *The Fourteenth Simenon Omnibus* (Penguin 4675, 1975); Harvest 138, 1983.

Plot: René Josselin, a quiet retired man, is killed in his home by two bullets. His son-in-law, who had spent part of the evening with him, had left him alone. Maigret begins to suspect that the murderer is someone close to the old man, and investigates the situations of the widow Francine, and his younger brother, who has lead a dissolute life and has frequently pressed René for money. Maigret eventually discovers the criminal, to whom a rather rough justice is meted out.

Comment: The novel reveals Maigret adopting a slightly different approach: rather than focusing on the psychology of the murderer, he seeks to discover the weak spot in the life of a middle class family. 3/5

63) Maigret And The Saturday Caller

(*Maigret et le client du Samedi*, 1962). Hamilton, 1964; Penguin 2638, 1968; in *Maigret Victorious* (Hamilton, 1975).

Plot: The owner of a small decorating business, Léonard Planchon, a nervous man with a harelip, has tried to call on Maigret regularly on a Saturday, to no avail. He finally tracks him down at his home and reveals that he plans to murder both his wife, Renée, and her lover, who is the foreman of the business. Maigret promises to help, but one day later Planchon has disappeared, and Maigret feels that Renée and her lover must know something about the affair. Then Maigret discovers a document which appears to be forged, and which provides a motive for murder.

Comments: It is Maigret's sympathy for the victim that drives the investigation. As in so many cases he comes up against the examining magistrate, who has little sympathy for his methods. 4/5

64) Maigret And The Dosser

(*Maigret et le clochard*, 1963). Hamilton, 1973; in *The Twelfth Simenon Omnibus* (Penguin 4431, 1977). Also translated as *Maigret And The Bum* (Harcourt, USA, 1973; Harvest 130, USA, 1982).

Plot: Some boatmen on the Seine pull out a badly injured tramp from the water. Maigret tries to find the owners of a red car that was observed near the scene, but it does not yield any leads. Subsequently it turns out that the tramp used to be a doctor, who had decided to get away from it all. When the man has recovered he tells Maigret that he witnessed a murder, which is why someone tried to kill him. There is an ironical twist when the murderer is finally discovered.

Comments: One of the most interesting aspects of this novel is the character of the doctor who became a tramp, and it provides a further example of the theme of flight, which characterizes many of the 'romans durs'. 5/5

65) Maigret Loses His Temper

(*La colère de Maigret*, 1963). Hamilton, 1965; Penguin 2701, 1967; Harcourt, USA, 1974; Harvest, USA, 1980.

Plot: The owner of a cabaret, Emile Boulay, is found strangled. He seems to have been leading a normal family life, but Maigret discovers that he had recently withdrawn a large sum of money from his account, and that he had encountered some shady dealings. For this knowledge he was silenced.

Comments: The reason Maigret loses his temper is that someone associated his name directly with a case of corruption. 3/5

66) Maigret And The Ghost

(*Maigret et le fantôme*, 1964). Hamilton, 1976. In a volume of three novels under the title *Maigret And The Ghost* (Penguin 4676, 1982). Also translated as *Maigret And The Apparition* (Harcourt, USA, 1976; Harvest 127, USA, 1980).

Plot: Maigret wakes to the news that the hapless Inspector Lognon has just escaped an attempt on his life. He had been conducting a surveillance of a couple, Norris Jonker, an art collector, and his wife Mireille. A young beautician has also disappeared. The only clue that Maigret has is a single word that Lognon was able to utter as he was brought out of the operating room: 'ghost'. Maigret eventually discovers that he is dealing with art forgers and attempted blackmail.

Comments: This novel is not highly regarded by some connoisseurs. But then the interest of a Simenon work is always in the detail. 2/5

67) Maigret On The Defensive

(*Maigret se défend*, 1964). Hamilton, 1966; Penguin 2831, 1968; Harcourt, USA, 1981.

Plot: Maigret is awakened at night by a telephone call from the daughter, Nicole Prieur, of a high government official. She is in a panic. After listening to her he settles her in a small hotel for the night. The next day he is summoned by the prefect of police because the young girl has accused him of attempting to seduce her. His job is on the line and he is suspended from duty. He becomes suspicious of a dentist, who is an acquaintance of the young woman, and Maigret decides it is time he had a check up on his teeth! It turns out that his investigation of another crime is being misinterpreted, and someone is trying to push him away.

Comments: Apart from being a rather unusual case, this novel also presents an intriguing portrait of a very intelligent murderer. 5/5

68) The Patience Of Maigret

(*La patience de Maigret*, 1965). Hamilton, 1966; in *The Second Simenon Omnibus* (Penguin 3185, 1970); in *Maigret: A Fifth Omnibus* (Hamilton, 1973). Also translated as *Maigret Bides His Time* (Harcourt, USA, 1985; Harvest 151, 1986).

Plot: An underworld contact of Maigret's, Manuel Palmari, who has been tracked by the police for about twenty years but whom they could never manage to convict, is found murdered. Maigret knew him to be behind a network of jewel robberies, but could never catch him. In the course of his investigation Maigret questions all the inhabitants of the apartment block, and discovers some interesting links between them, but not in time to prevent another death.

Comments: Considered rightly a classic Maigret case, with evocative descriptions of Paris. 5/5

69) Maigret And The Nahour Case

(*Maigret et l'affaire Nahour*, 1967). Hamilton, 1967; in *The First Simenon Omnibus* (Penguin 3184, 1970); Harcourt, USA, 1982; Harvest, USA, 1986.

Plot: Maigret is summoned in the middle of the night by his friend Dr. Pardon, who has been looking after a woman who was lightly wounded by a gunshot as she was about to take a flight for Amsterdam. In the morning a wealthy Lebanese gambler, Felix Nahour, is found murdered in a hotel room. Maigret discovers that the two cases are connected. The wounded woman, Lina, is Nahour's wife, who was trying to run off with her young lover, Alvaredo. Nahour's secretary, Fouad Ouéni, also seems to play a sinister role in the affair.

Comments: As with so many of the novels the strength of this one lies in the psychological study of the murderer. 4/5

70) Maigret's Pickpocket

(*Le voleur de Maigret*, 1967). Hamilton, 1968; Harcourt, USA, 1968; in *The Second Simenon Omnibus* (Penguin 3185, 1970). Also translated as *Maigret And The Pickpocket* (Harvest, USA, 1985).

Plot: While traveling on a bus Maigret has his wallet stolen, but the following day the pickpocket contacts him. He proves to be a journalist and would-be screenplay writer who is suspected of the murder of his wife and who wants Maigret to prove his innocence. Maigret mingles in the world of filmmakers, discovering that the wife had been the lover of a film director. He follows several false trails but arrives finally at the simple truth.

Comments: Many feel that this is not one of the best Maigrets, but there is good characterization to enjoy. 3/5

71) Maigret Takes The Waters

(*Maigret à Vichy*, 1968). Hamilton, 1969; in *Maigret: A Fifth Omnibus* (Hamilton, 1973); in *The Seventh Simenon Omnibus* (Penguin 3838, 1974). Also translated as *Maigret in Vichy* (Harcourt, USA, 1969; Harvest 140, USA, 1984).

Plot: While Maigret is taking the cure at Vichy, a middle-aged woman of independent means, Hélène Lange, is murdered. The local chief of police is an old acquaintance of Maigret and asks him to help solve the mystery. The woman's sister tells them that Hélène had a lover but hides some facts about their background. Maigret uncovers a case of deception that goes back many years.

Comments: The atmosphere of Vichy is charmingly evoked. Madame Maigret proves to be very helpful in this case. 4/5

72) Maigret Hesitates

(*Maigret hésite*, 1968). Hamilton, 1970; Harcourt, USA, 1970; in *The Eighth Simenon Omnibus* (Penguin 3897, 1975); Harvest 152, USA, 1986.

Plot: Maigret is warned by an anonymous letter that a crime is going to be committed. When he investigates the household of the lawyer Parendon, nothing appears to be out of order, except that the couple do not get on very well. But three days later the lawyer's secretary is found with her throat cut. Maigret reproaches himself for not being able to prevent the murder.

Comments: Memorable for its evocation of Paris in springtime, and its account of an unhappy love. 5/5

73) Maigret's Boyhood Friend

(*L'ami d'enfance de Maigret*, 1968). Hamilton, 1970; Harcourt, USA, 1970; in *The Fifth Simenon Omnibus* (Penguin 3432, 1972); Harvest 131, USA, 1981.

Plot: A former school-friend of Maigret, Léon Florentin, seeks Maigret's help: his mistress Josée has been murdered. Maigret discovers that she had four other gentleman friends, who supported her financially, but that Florentin was her special lover. Although Florentin pretends to commit suicide and tells many lies, Maigret does not believe he is capable of murder. It seems however that he tried blackmailing one of Josée's gentlemen.

Comments: Maigret is hampered rather than helped by the presence of someone he knows from his schooldays, and had never really liked very much anyway. 4/5

74) Maigret And The Killer

(*Maigret et le tueur*, 1969). Hamilton, 1971; Harcourt, USA, 1971; in *The Seventh Simenon Omnibus* (Penguin 3838, 1974); Harvest 124, USA, 1979.

Plot: A young student, who hangs around seedy bars and has a passion for recording the conversations he has, is murdered. An anonymous caller claims responsibility for the murder. Maigret tries to make contact, to persuade the person to come forward. Then he finds he has a pathological killer on his hands.

Comments: The strength of the novel is in its depiction of a pathological mind. 4/5

75) Maigret And The Wine Merchant

(*Maigret et le marchand de vin*, 1970). Hamilton, 1971; Harcourt, USA, 1971; in *The Sixth Simenon Omnibus* (Penguin 3542, 1972); Harvest 125, USA, 1960.

Plot: One of the richest wine merchants in Paris, Oscar Chabut, is found dead outside an elegant house used for the purpose of discreet sexual rendez-vous. Maigret discovers that the man's family is not particularly grieved at their loss. It seems like an act of jealousy among rivals. It is when Maigret investigates some of the reasons why Chabut was generally disliked that it becomes obvious who the killer was.

Comments: The focus of the novel is on the psychology of humiliation, and how it can turn to anger and an act of revenge. 4/5

76) Maigret And The Madwoman

(*La folle de Maigret*, 1970). Hamilton, 1972; Harcourt, USA, 1972; in *The Tenth Simenon Omnibus* (Penguin 3665, 1976); Harvest, USA, 1979.

Plot: An old woman, Léontine, is not taken seriously by the police when she complains that someone seems to be persecuting her. She is continually finding household items shifted around. But then she is found dead. Maigret can find no obvious clues, though there is evidence of there having been a firearm in the house. Attention is focused on the old lady's niece, Angèle, and her lover, who has connections with some gangsters. A very unusual revolver is at the heart of the mystery.

Comments: Critics are divided about this novel: some find it lacks verisimilitude, while Edmund Crispin declared it 'one of the very best of the recent Maigret stories'. 4/5

77) Maigret And The Loner

(*Maigret et l'homme tout seul*, 1971). Hamilton, 1975; Harcourt, USA, 1975; in *The Thirteenth Simenon Omnibus* (Penguin 4511, 1978); Harvest 139, USA, 1983.

Plot: A tramp with well-manicured nails, Marcel Vivien, is killed in a dere-lict house in Les Halles district of Paris. The man's wife proves hostile to Maigret's attempts to unravel the past of this former cabinet-maker. He discovers that the man had given up everything for the sake of a young girl called Nina, who then left him for a man called Mahossier. There then followed a chain of events that lasted over twenty years, resulting eventually in Vivien's death.

Comments: As is the case in many other novels Simenon was clearly more interested in the life of a man who gave up his ordinary life for an ideal than in the resolution of the murder mystery. 5/5

78) Maigret And The Flea

(*Maigret et l'indicateur*, 1971). Hamilton, 1972; in *The Eighth Simenon Omnibus* (Penguin 3897, 1975). Also translated as *Maigret And The Informer* (Harcourt, USA, 1973).

Plot: A restaurant owner in Montmartre, Maurice Marcia, with gangland connections, is murdered. Maigret has had his suspicions about him for a long time but has not been able to prove anything. He finally gets a tip-off from an informer, who is eventually identified as a former pimp. The information proves to be reliable.

Comments: The novel is noteworthy for the introduction of a new character among the inspectors: a certain Inspector Louis, widowed, dressed in black and melancholy, but who knows his district well. In some ways it can be said that Maigret does not really solve the mystery. If it had not been for the informer, he might never have made any headway. 3/5

79) Maigret And Monsieur Charles

(*Maigret et Monsieur Charles*, 1972). Hamilton, 1973; in *The Ninth Simenon Omnibus* (Penguin 3980, 1976).

Plot: Rather belatedly Nathalie Sabin-Levesque asks Maigret to find her husband, who has been missing for over a month. He investigates the family situation and discovers that husband and wife did not get on at all well. The husband, Gérard, spent much of his free time in bars and cabarets, where he was well known and liked as 'Monsieur Charles' ('a young man who would never grow old'). Meanwhile his wife had become completely dependent on alcohol and was also deceiving her husband with a barman called Jo Fazio. Then Gérard's body is fished out of the Seine. Gradually Maigret unravels a sad story of two ruined lives.

Comments: The revelation of the truth is brought about not by deduction or even interrogation but by Maigret putting his psychological insight to practical use and putting pressure on the suspect to act rashly. This was to be not only the last of the Maigret series but the last novel that Simenon wrote. Thereafter he devoted himself to dictating his memoirs. It is a fitting and accomplished end to the Maigret series. 5/5

4 The 'Romans Durs'

The term 'roman dur' (plural: 'romans durs'), which was used by Simenon himself to refer to all those novels that he regarded as his real literary works, is difficult to render precisely in English. This is because its meaning in French is also not precise. Just calling them Simenon's 'serious' novels is clearly inadequate, because it suggests that there must be something 'not serious' about the Maigret novels.

The word 'roman' translates easily enough as 'novel', but of the various possible meanings of 'dur' ('hard', 'tough', 'heavy', 'hard-going', 'harrowing' etc), one alone is not suitable to describe all the Simenon novels. What Simenon was probably trying to suggest is that these novels reflect disturbing aspects of life in a frank and unflinching way. As he was using a term that he had coined, it seems wisest to retain the French expression. There are precedents enough in the field of appreciation of the arts ('film noir,' 'art nouveau,' 'montage' etc). So 'roman dur' it is.

Checklist Of 'Romans Durs'

1) The Man From Everywhere

(*Le Relais d'Alsace*, 1931). In *Maigret And M. Labbé* (Routledge, 1941; Harcourt, USA, 1942); together with another novel in *The Man From Everywhere And Newhaven-Dieppe* (Penguin 855, 1952).

Plot: In a quiet Alsatian village a crime is committed for which a notorious international criminal known as 'The Commodore' is thought to be responsible. He was hoping to find anonymity in this situation, but he cannot escape from his former identity. M. Labbé of the Paris Sûreté arrives, but he finds he is no real match for the master criminal.

Comments: This was the first novel without the character of Maigret that was written under Simenon's real name. It is regarded by many as a classic. 5/5

2) The Mystery Of The 'Polarlys'

(*Le passager du 'Polarlys'*, 1932). In *In Two Latitudes* (Routledge, 1942; Penguin 828, 1952).

Plot: The story takes place on board a thousand-ton steamer, the 'Polarlys', which travels between Hamburg and Kirkenes in Norway. The voyage begins with the mysterious murder of a young Parisian woman, Marie Baron, and as the voyage progresses amid northern blizzards, the Norwegian captain feels that the evil eye is on his ship.

Comments: Although Maigret is not present, many have felt that it has many of the characteristics of a Maigret novel. 4/5

3) The House By The Canal

(*La maison du canal*, 1933). With another novel in *The House By The Canal* (Routledge Kegan Paul, 1952).

Plot: The story takes place in the small village of Neeroeteren, in Belgium, near to the border with Holland, in the province of Limbourg. A young orphan girl goes to live with her cousins in the village. While one of the cousins is trying to embrace the girl he accidentally kills a young boy. Two other tragic incidents follow.

Comments: This novel is particularly fascinating due to the fact that it takes place in Simenon's mother's birthplace. 3/5

4) Mr. Hire's Engagement

(*Les fiançailles de M. Hire*, 1933). In *The Sacrifice* (Hamilton, 1956); in *A Simenon Omnibus* (Hamilton, 1956); Arrow, 1958.

Plot: A young woman has been found murdered in the Villejuif area of Paris, and the police soon suspect a man who lives alone not far from the scene of the crime. This is Monsieur Hire, who has already been in prison on a vice charge, and has made a living in various dubious ways. He spies on a young woman in the room opposite and gradually develops strong feelings for her. He also discovers that the real murderer is none other than the girl's boyfriend. He dreams of marrying her and escaping to Switzerland. But the novel ends tragically.

Comments: A brilliantly conceived and written novel, from the perspective of its protagonist. The evocations of Parisian streets and bars are powerfully but economically realised through details of sounds, light and smells. 5/5

5) Tropic Moon

(*Le coup de lune*, 1933). In *In Two Latitudes* (Routledge, 1942; Penguin 828, 1952); Harcourt, 1943; in *African Trio* (Hamilton, 1979; Harcourt, USA, 1979).

Plot: The novel takes place in Libreville, French Equatorial Africa. A mild young man, Joseph Timar, who is new to the continent, gets involved with Adèle, who has a dubious past. She is a ruthless but good-hearted woman. She has however killed a young Negro.

Comments: There is a clear critique in this novel of French colonialist rule and its willingness to twist the facts to defend itself. 4/5

6) The Window Over The Way

(*Les gens d'en face*, 1933). With another novel in *The Window Over The Way* (Routledge Kegan Paul, 1951). In a new translation as *Window Over The Way* (Penguin 2363, 1966).

Plot: Set in the USSR this novel tells of a Turkish diplomat, Adil Bey, who, on a mission to Batoum, becomes convinced that his soviet secretary Sonia is trying to poison him, and that she is acting on official orders. The problem is that he is very much attracted to her.

Comments: The novel is fascinating for its unusual setting and cast of characters. 3/5

7) The Night Club

(*L'Âne Rouge*, 1933). Hamilton, 1979; Harcourt, USA, 1979; with two other novels in *Maigret's Rival* (Penguin 5468, 1985).

Plot: Situated in Nantes, the novel focuses on the life in a nightclub called 'L'Âne Rouge' ('The Red Donkey'). A young journalist, Jean Cholet, hangs around there among second-rate artists and gets to know a young woman called Lulu, who sings in the club. He drinks to forget his restrictive family life, with a pathetic mother who is always complaining and a father whom he regards as a failure. But when his father suddenly dies it provokes an unexpected crisis in his life.

Comments: This a fascinating source for themes in Simenon's own life, and many aspects of the novel are autobiographical, especially the character of the young journalist fascinated by the seedy aspects of life, with a weak mother and a father who unexpectedly dies. The difference is that the story is set in Nantes and not Liège. 3/5

8) The Woman Of The Grey House

(*Le haut mal*, 1933). In *Affairs Of Destiny* (Routledge, 1942; Harcourt, USA, 1945).

Plot: Germaine Pontreau has her heart set on owning the property that has just been inherited by her son-in-law, Jean Nalliers. She has decided to get rid of him, whom she regards as just a nobody, and pushes him from a window of their farm. She then covers up the crime as an accident, which she is able to do convincingly because Jean suffered from epilepsy ('le haut mal' of the French title). Suspicions are however aroused.

Comments: This novel is part murder mystery and part a study in criminal psychology. 3/5

9) Newhaven-Dieppe

(*L'homme de Londres*, 1934). In *Affairs of Destiny* (Routledge, 1942; Harcourt, USA, 1945). And with another novel in *The Man From Everywhere And Newhaven-Dieppe* (Penguin 855, 1952).

Plot: Louis Maloin is signalman at Dieppe harbour station. From his signal-box he can watch both the trawlers out at sea and the movements of people in the town. One evening he witnesses a murder take place directly below him on the quayside. He goes to investigate and manages to get hold of the suitcase that the murderer has stolen from his victim. It is full of money. From that moment on he is involved in a way that will lead him also to commit violence.

Comments: This is really classic Simenon, with that port atmosphere of which he was obviously fond. 5/5

10) The Lodger

(*Le locataire*, 1934). In *Escape In Vain* (Routledge, 1943; Harcourt, USA, 1944; Penguin 830, 1952; Harcourt, USA, 1983).

Plot: A Turkish tobacco exporter, Elie Nagéar, is travelling to Brussels and during the voyage he becomes the lover of a young woman, Sylvie Baron, who has been working in cabaret in Cairo. In Brussels his business does not do at all well and he kills a rich Dutchman and robs him. He then goes to join Sylvie and her mother at Charleroi. The mother finds out what Elie has done and cannot understand how a man like him could have resorted to murder.

Comments: The psychological study of the murderer is the main focus of this novel. 5/5

11) One Way Out

(*Les suicidés*, 1934). In *Escape In Vain* (Routledge, 1943; Penguin 830, 1952; Harcourt, USA, 1944).

Plot: The novel recounts the story of a young bank clerk and his seventeen year-old girlfriend, who cannot get married because of his poor financial situation. The girl's father is very hostile towards him, and this provokes him to set fire to the man's house. The couple flee to Paris, but more disasters follow, and they feel that the only true escape for them is in suicide (as indeed the original French title made clear from the start).

Comments: One of those truly bleak Simenon novels that merit the term 'roman dur'. 3/5

12) A Wife At Sea

(*Les Pitard*, 1935). In a volume with another novel, *A Wife At Sea And The Murderer* (Routledge Kegan Paul, 1949).

Plot: The captain and owner of the freighter 'Le Tonnerre-de-Dieu' (meaning in French, rather dramatically, 'God's Thunder') is setting out on his first voyage in the newly acquired vessel. Commander Lannec has bought it with money provided by his wife and mother-in-law. They are making their way from Rouen to Reykjavik. His wife Matthilde (whose maiden name is Pitard, as in the original French title) has insisted on being on board, but she has a rather abusive manner and in the narrow confines of the ship this soon leads to tension between them. The weather gets bad and Lannec cannot stand the way his wife treats him any more. To make it worse his wife accuses him of just marrying her to get the Pitards' money. This all leads to a tragic conclusion.

Comments: Simenon has used many of his own experiences of seafaring in these northern waters. 3/5

13) The Disintegration of J.P.G.

(*L'évadé*, 1936). Routledge, 1937.

Plot: A German teacher in a school in La Rochelle suddenly starts behaving oddly and worries those around him. Just recently he has started to spend a lot of time in local cafés with a young manicurist from a local hairdresser's. It turns out that Guillaume is an ex-convict who was arrested for murder and that the girl, Mado, is a prostitute who helped him to escape from Guyana. The teacher is completely distraught by the situation, and fears discovery by the police. He also feels he could not cope with the family crisis that would ensue if the truth came out. He seeks to avoid the situation by fleeing to Paris.

Comments: It is a pity that the novel has not been more readily available, as it treats of the theme of an extreme state of mind, which Simenon has evoked very successfully in some of his best novels. 4/5

14) The Long Exile

(*Long cours*, 1936). Hamilton, 1983; Harcourt, USA, 1983.

Plot: A young woman, Charlotte Godebieu has killed her former lover and employer and decides to flee with a friend, Joseph Mittel, to Buenaventura. They get a passage on board a freighter used by smugglers. The long journey is difficult, especially for Joseph, who has been relegated to the boiler room. But Charlotte soon manages to improve her status by becoming the captain's mistress. Captain Mopps leaves them both to their fate in Columbia, where they have to survive among the natives. To add to their concerns Charlotte discovers she is pregnant. A change comes in their lives with the arrival of a letter from Captain Mopps, but it is not all to be for the good.

Comments: The plot is reminiscent of some of the popular novels which Simenon used to churn out before Maigret made him famous. 2/5

15) The Breton Sisters

(*Les demoiselles de Concarneau*, 1936). In *Havoc By Accident* (Routledge, 1943; Harcourt, USA, 1943; Penguin 829, 1952). Also with another novel in *The Man Who Watched The Trains Go By And The Breton Sisters* (Penguin 7979, 1986).

Plot: A rich fisherman, Jules Guérec, driving home after enjoying himself in a nearby town, knocks down a little boy, who subsequently dies. He flees the scene of the accident and is too afraid to tell the police or admit it to his two sisters. Torn by guilt he attempts to help the boy's family financially without telling the mother that he was responsible. Eventually he even thinks of marrying the mother but comes up against the opposition of his two sisters, one of whom guessed the truth about what happened and tells the boy's mother. Guérec can no longer cope with the strain.

Comments: The novel deals with a theme to be found in several other Simenon novels: the results of attempting to avoid responsibility for a crime. 3/5

16) Aboard The Aquitaine

(*45° à l'ombre*, 1936). In *African Trio* (Hamilton, 1979; Harcourt, USA, 1979).

Plot: The novel takes place on board the liner 'Aquitaine' which plies between the Congo and Bordeaux. Dr. Donadieu is the resident doctor on board and enjoys observing the lives of the passengers who make up a microcosm of colonial society. There is no real plot as such in this novel, which consists of a series of incidents, such as a child's illness, the behaviour of one of the officers, an affair between a steward and a passenger, etc.

Comments: The main interest of this novel is in its depiction of the decline of French colonial society, seen from the point of view of the doctor. 3/5

17) The Shadow Falls

(*Le testament Donadieu*, 1937). Routledge, 1945; Harcourt, USA, 1945.

Plot: The novel plots the decline and break up of a family after the death of the old ship owner, Oscar Donadieu (no relation to the doctor of the same name in the previous novel *Aboard the Aquitaine*). His body is found in a pool in the port of La Rochelle, and murder is not ruled out. His four children and wife are surprised by the terms of his will: none of them will inherit anything until the last of them comes of age. So from then on the various family members fight for control of the family business. The family begins to disintegrate under a sequence of scandals, malpractices and attempts to settle scores. At the end the youngest child, named after the old man, but known to all as Kiki, and who has been in the background all along, returns. He has rejected everything that the family stands for.

Comments: This is Simenon's longest novel, and one of the few in which he endeavours to depict a whole range of characters with equal intensity. Characters who appear at the beginning to be secondary come into their own eventually. His sense of atmosphere and place never fail him. At times the behaviour of some members of the family borders on farce, but it is the absurdity of the 'human comedy' that is being depicted, which is why perhaps this novel, more than any other of his works, has been often compared to the work of Balzac. It is well overdue for a reprint. 5/5

18) The Murderer

(*L'assassin*, 1937). With another novel in *A Wife At Sea* (Routledge Kegan Paul, 1949); Penguin 1223, 1958; Harcourt, USA, 1986.

Plot: A forty five-year-old doctor in the Dutch town of Sneek decides to murder his wife and her lover, a lawyer, and then commit suicide. He manages to kill the couple but not himself. He puts it around that the couple have run off together. He then quite openly conducts an affair with his servant, Neel. But when the bodies are discovered suspicion naturally falls on him. There is, however, no real evidence against him. As time goes by the servant takes the place of his wife and the local inhabitants avoid him. The doctor has to face the emptiness of his life.

Comments: The novel is utterly compelling. The reader sees everything from the point of the view of the murderer. Simenon at his most accomplished. 5/5

19) Talatala

(*Le blanc à lunettes*, 1937). In *Havoc By Accident* (Routledge, 1943; Harcourt, USA, 1943; Penguin 829, 1952). In *African Trio* (Hamilton, 1979; Harcourt, USA, 1979).

Plot: A French coffee planter, Ferdinand Graux, nicknamed by the natives 'Talatala' ('the white man with the spectacles') owns a plantation in the Belgian Congo. He has been leading a quiet solitary life until one day a private aeroplane is forced to make a landing nearby. The wife of an English diplomat, a certain Lady Makinson, is on board, and he falls in love with her, abandoning completely his fiancée back in France. The scene changes to Istanbul, but the novel ends back in the Congo again.

Comments: Unusually for Simenon, the novel ends with a man who was overcome with passion, coming to his senses at last. 3/5

20) Home Town

(*Faubourg*, 1937). In *On The Danger Line* (Routledge, 1944; Harcourt, USA, 1944; Penguin 858, 1952).

Plot: After an absence of twenty-four years, René de Ritter, who has had various dealings with the underworld, returns to his home town in the company of Léa, a prostitute. At first he does not reveal his identity, but soon starts visiting members of his family and other acquaintances to try and squeeze money out of them. He even marries a woman he had known formerly, while the prostitute has an affair with the hotel owner. This casual lifestyle is doomed to end in tragedy.

Comments: The novel blends straight narration with flashbacks. 3/5

21) Blind Path

(*Chemin sans issue*, 1938). In *Lost Moorings* (Routledge, 1946; Penguin 857, 1952).

Plot: Two young white Russians have a close friendship dating back to the October Revolution. One day one of them is attracted to a woman, which leads to the break up of their friendship.

Comments: The focus is on the friendship of the two men. The final scene, in a night shelter in Warsaw, between Vladimir and the young Caucasian, whom he has betrayed, is very impressively realised. 4/5

22) The Survivors

(*Les rescapés du 'Télémaque*, 1938). With another novel in *Black Rain* (Routledge Kegan Paul, 1949; Penguin 2246; Harcourt, USA, 1985).

Plot: Pierre and Charles Canut are the sons of a sailor who died in a shipwreck many years before. The last survivor of the incident is murdered, and it seems that Pierre, a popular local captain of a trawler, will be charged with committing the crime. Charles tries to discover the identity of the murderer.

Comments: The style is often reminiscent of a Maigret mystery, though the master investigator is absent. 3/5

23) The Green Thermos

(*Le suspect*, 1938). In *On The Danger Line* (Routledge, 1944; Harcourt, USA, 1944; Penguin 858, 1952).

Plot: A moderate anarchist, Pierre Chave, tries to persuade a younger friend to give up his plan to blow up an aircraft factory at Courbevoie.

Comments: Terrorism is not a common theme in Simenon's writings.Tthe atmosphere of contemporary anarchist circles in Paris is well described. 3/5

24) Poisoned Relations

(*Les sœurs Lacroix*, 1938). With another novel in *Poisoned Relations* (Routledge Kegan Paul, 1950); Penguin 1224, 1958.

Plot: Two sisters, Mathilde and Léopoldine Lacroix, live together in a house in Bayeux. One is married and the other is a widow, but they both love the same man, the husband of Mathilde. The atmosphere of the household is full of hatred and mistrust, and the children live in a constant state of fear. It does not come as a surprise to read that someone has discovered arsenic in the soup.

Comments: A harrowing story with scarcely one likeable character, but which draws the reader on by a compulsive need to know what is going to happen. 5/5

25) Banana Tourist

(*Touriste de Bananes*, 1938). In *Lost Moorings* (Routledge, 1946; Penguin 857, 1952).

Plot: This novel is in fact a sequel to *The Shadow Falls*. Young Oscar Donadieu (known as Kiki in the first novel) is on his way to Tahiti, after rejecting all that his dead father stood for. In Tahiti he lives in a remote abandoned hut with a Tahitian prostitute, Tamatéa. He becomes revolted by the life of the colonial community in Tahiti, and gradually becomes disillusioned too with his own attempt to return to nature.

Comments: This is the only novel that Simenon ever wrote as a sequel (if one leaves out of account some of the Maigret novels). It only reinforces the pessimism of the original novel. In a way the title says it all: 'Banana Tourist' was the nickname the local people gave to those idealists who came to the island in search of a simple life close to nature. 3/5

26) Monsieur La Souris

(*Monsieur La Souris*, 1938). In *Poisoned Relations* (Routledge Kegan Paul, 1950). New translation as *The Mouse* (Penguin 2378, 1966).

Plot: A tramp nicknamed 'Monsieur La Souris' (literally 'Mr Mouse') finds a sum of money near a corpse and hands it over to the police, without giving any further details of how he found it. He hopes that he will get the money back again if it is not claimed.

Comments: The story is pure Maigret in spirit. The outcome is unique amongst Simenon's works. 4/5

27) Chit Of A Girl

(*La Marie du port*, 1938). With another novel in *Chit Of A Girl* (Routledge Kegan Paul, 1949). Retitled as *Girl In Waiting* in *Girl In Waiting* (Pan, 1957).

Plot: Marie le Flem is the daughter of a fisherman, who has just died in Port-en-Bessin. She gets a job as a waitress in a local café. She is generally bad-tempered, but shrewd and determined to get what she wants. Her older sister, Odile, is more good-natured. Her sister's lover, Chatelard, is the owner of the café and a local cinema in Cherbourg. He believes he can easily win Marie's affections too, but she is coolly indifferent to him. He teases and taunts her, all to no avail. Complications ensue when Marcel, a new admirer of both girls, arrives on the scene.

Comments: The novel is attractive for the atmospheric description of a fishing port, for which Simenon is so famous. 3/5

28) The Man Who Watched The Trains Go By

(*L'homme qui regardait passer les trains*, 1938). Routledge, 1942; Pan, 1948; Penguin 2150, 1964; Also in *The Man Who Watched The Trains Go By And The Breton Sisters* (Penguin 7979, 1986).

Plot: Kees Popinga lives in Groningen, Holland, with his wife and two children. He is thirty-nine years old. One day his boss confides in him that the firm is bankrupt and that he is going to quietly disappear. Popinga decides to leave his wife and family, and then tries to seduce the mistress of his former boss, but is driven to murder her when she makes fun of him. From then on the novel follows Popinga's progress as he goes to Paris and mixes with various dubious and criminal people and traces his inevitable decline.

Comments: One of Simenon's classic flight novels. 5/5

29) The White Horse Inn

(*Le Cheval-Blanc*, 1938). With two other novels in *The White Horse Inn* (Hamilton, 1980); Harcourt, USA, 1980.

Plot: The Arbelet family stays at the White Horse Inn in Pouilly and discovers that an old watchman is one of Monsieur Arbelet's uncles.

Comments: The novel's main interest is in its depiction of the local culture. 2/5

30) Chez Krull

(*Chez Krull*, 1939). In *A Sense Of Guilt* (Hamilton, 1955); Four Square, 1958; in *The Second Simenon Omnibus* (Hamilton, 1974).

Plot: A German cousin of the Krull family, Hans, arrives at the family home, which is above the family grocery business. The corpse of a young girl is found in the canal. Hans seduces the young daughter of the family and is suspected by the community of having killed the girl found in the canal, but suspicion soon passes to his studious cousin Joseph.

Comments: A disturbing novel of a family, which is very insecure because of its essential foreignness. Hans unsettles them all even more, and they clearly all want him to leave. Its theme of the scapegoat has broader cultural and social implications. A novel worth seeking out. 5/5

31) The Burgomaster of Furnes

(*Le bourgmestre de Furnes*, 1939). Routledge Kegan Paul, 1952.

Plot: The burgomaster of Furnes, Joris Terlinck, is a strong, authoritarian figure. A young man, to whom he refused to give any money, commits suicide. Many ordeals that he suffers do not soften and humanise him: his wife is very ill and dies; his daughter suffers from a mental illness and is finally put into a mental hospital; and the local council are firmly opposed to him. But he does not yield.

Comments: A fascinating psychological study. It is indeed a pity that editions of this work are not more readily available. 4/5

32) The Family Lie

(*Malempin*, 1940). Hamilton, 1978; Harcourt, USA, 1976.

Plot: Dr Malempin, who works in Paris, is preparing to leave on his holidays, but discovers that his son has an attack of diphtheria. While watching over his son during his illness the doctor recalls his own past and especially his relationship with his own father.

Comments: A warm and affectionate study, rare for Simenon. 4/5

33) The Strangers In The House

(*Les inconnus dans la maison*, 1940). Routledge Kegan Paul, 1951. Translated as *Strangers In The House* (Doubleday, USA, 1954; Signet, 1957). New translation as *Stranger in The House* (Penguin 2732, 1967).

Plot: A former lawyer, Hector Loursat, has shut himself away from the world in a large house, where he spends his time getting drunk. One evening he hears a gunshot and finds a corpse in his attic. He learns from the examining magistrate that his daughter Nicole and her friend Emile Manu are somehow involved in the death of this stranger, who appears to be a criminal. When Emile is arrested Loursat decides to take on his defence and makes a brilliant speech defending the young generation and pointing out the parents' responsibility for their children.

Comments: A deservedly well-known novel, which deals with some important themes and includes a psychological study of alcoholism and the nature of parental responsibility. 5/5

34) Justice

(*Cour d'assises*, 1941). Included with another novel in *Chit Of A Girl* (Routledge Kegan Paul, 1949); and with the same other novel re-titled in *Girl In Waiting* (Pan, 1957); Harcourt, USA, 1985.

Plot: Petit Louis leads a life of petty crime. His speciality is conducting affairs with lonely, middle-aged women. He also gets involved in a gang's robbery of a post office. At the time of the story he is living with a mature wealthy woman and a young prostitute. But the girl's 'protector' comes out of prison, and Louis returns home to find the middle-aged woman murdered. In a panic he gets rid of the body, but the police are soon on his trail.

Comments: The processes of justice and the nature of guilt are central themes. A legal trial forms an important part of the novel. 4/5

35) The Country Doctor

(*Bergelon*, 1941). Included in *The White Horse Inn* (Hamilton, 1980); translated as *The Delivery* (Harcourt, USA, 1981).

Plot: Bergelon is a local doctor of no particular talents. One day he accepts an offer made to him by a certain Dr. Mandalin and he passes some of his patients on to Mandalin. But one of Mandalin's patients, a woman giving birth, and the child, die because Mandalin is drunk. The husband of the woman threatens to kill Bergelon, who then takes flight through France and Belgium.

Comments: Familiar Simenon themes of disappointment with life and attempts to escape from an unbearable reality. 3/5

36) The Outlaw

(*L'outlaw*, 1941). Hamilton, 1986; Harcourt, USA, 1987.

Plot: Two refugees from Central Europe, Stan and Nouchi, are desperately looking for work in Paris. Stan hits upon the idea of tipping off the police about a Polish gang of criminals in order get the reward, but it does not work. Despair finally drives Stan to murder.

Comments: The story of a rather sad hopeless plight. 3/5

37) Black Rain

(*Il pleut Bergère*, 1941). Reynal, 1947; with another novel in *Black Rain* (Routledge Kegan Paul, 1949; Penguin 2246, 1965).

Plot: Jerôme Lecoeur recalls his childhood in a small village in Normandy at the end of the nineteenth century, telling the story of his family and the search for an anarchist.

Comments: Told in the first person. Some have found similarities with the autobiographical novel *Pedigree*. 4/5

38) Strange Inheritance

(*Le voyager de la Toussaint*, 1941). Routledge Kegan Paul, 1950.

Plot: The young Gilles Mauvoisin returns to La Rochelle on the eve of All Saints Day ('Toussaint') after the recent accidental death of his parents. He inherits his uncle's business, but is disgusted to discover all the scheming that has been going on in the family. He decides to escape abroad with the young widow, Colette, of his uncle.

Comments: The novel is close in theme, treatment and setting to *The Shadow Falls*. The central character Gilles is also comparable to Kiki in that novel. 3/5

39) Ticket Of Leave

(*La Veuve Couderc*, 1942). Routledge Kegan Paul, 1954; Penguin 2314, 1965; translated as *The Widow* in *The Magician And The Widow* (Doubleday, USA, 1955).

Plot: Jean has been released from prison after serving five years for murder. He gets a job as a farmhand with a widow called Mme Couderc, who is known as Tati. She lives together with her old father-in-law who lets her run the farm in return for sexual favours. Jean also becomes her lover but is soon attracted to a young girl living nearby, called Félicie. Uncontrollable jealousy and violence erupt.

Comments: André Gide compared the novel to Camus' *L'étranger*. Jean is also a man who can never overcome his strangeness in the community. It is indeed a stunning accomplishment, not least for its vivid descriptions of country life and atmosphere. One has the feeling that no word is superfluous. 5/5

40) Young Cardinaud

(*Le fils Cardinaud*, 1942). In *The Sacrifice* (Hamilton, 1956); Four Square, 1959.

Plot: Hubert Cardinaud returns to his house one Sunday after church to find that his wife Marthe has left him, taking the housekeeping money with her, but leaving their two children in his care. Cardinaud sets out to find her, and discovers that she has gone off with a rather disreputable individual.

Comments: Yet another novel about flight, but this time from the point of view of the person left behind. A central theme is also that of the problem of human communication.4/5

41) The Trial Of Bébé Donge

(*La vérité sur Bébé Donge*, 1942). Routledge Kegan Paul, 1952; Ace, 1960. Also translated as *I Take This Woman* in *Satan's Children* (Prentice, 1953; Signet, 1953).

Plot: Mme. Donge, who is known by the nickname Bébé, tries to poison her husband, François, with arsenic while they are staying in their country house. But the husband recovers and she is arrested for attempted murder. The husband tries to understand his wife's behaviour and reflects on their life together. Meanwhile Bébé is put on trial.

Comments: This is an unusual novel in that the crime leads to better understanding. Perhaps this is one of the reasons why this novel was published in 1999 in France in a special edition for secondary school pupils, with extensive critical commentaries. 4/5

42) The Little Doctor

Short stories. (*Le petit docteur*, 1943). Hamilton, 1978; Harcourt, USA, 1981.

Contents: 'The Doctor's Hunch' ('Le flair du petit docteur'); 'The Girl In Pale Blue'('La demoiselle en bleu pâle'); 'A Woman Screamed' ('Une femme a crié'); 'The Haunting Of Monsieur Marbe' ('Le fantôme de M. Marbe'); 'The Midwinter Marriage' (' Les mariés du 1er décembre'); 'The Corpse In The Kitchen Garden' ('La mort tombé du ciel'); 'The Dutchman's Luck' ('La bonne fortune du hollandais'); 'Popaul And His Negro' ('Le passager et son nègre'); 'The Trail Of The Red-Haired Man' ('La piste de l'homme roux'); 'The Disappearance Of The Admiral' ('L'amiral a disparu'); 'The Communication Cord' (' La sonnette d'alarme'); 'Arsenic Hall' ('Le château de l'arsenic'); 'Death In A Department Store' ('L'amoureux aux pantoufles'). 3/5

43) The Gendarme's Report

(*Le rapport du gendarme*, 1944). In *The Window Over The Way* (Routledge Kegan Paul, 1951).

Plot: A man is found badly wounded on a farm near Fontenay-le-Comte. He has also lost his memory. The reason for his presence is to seek out the Roy family, but he does not know why. The local policeman gradually discovers some secrets about the family, which leads to acts of violence.

Comments: A familiar mixture of police investigation and psychological insight. 3/5

44) Across The Street

(*La fenêtre des Rouet*, 1945). Routledge Kegan Paul, 1954.

Plot: An old spinster called Dominique has nothing better to do than spend her time watching what her neighbours are up to. One day she sees her neighbour, Antoinette Rouet, deliberately leave her husband in agony, when he is clearly suffering a heart attack. The young widow wastes no time in acquiring various lovers, and Dominique witnesses everything that is going on. But the whole affair makes Dominique acutely aware of the failure of her own life and leads to tragic consequences.

Comments: A sensitive study of a failed life. 4/5

45) Monsieur Monde Vanishes

(*La fuite de Monsieur Monde*, 1945). Hamilton, 1967; in *The First Simenon Omnibus* (Penguin 3184, 1970); Harcourt, USA, 1977; together with another novel in *The Little Man From Archangel And Monsieur Monde Vanishes* (Penguin 8139, 1986).

Plot: On his forty-eighth birthday Norbert Monde, head of a well-respected firm in Paris founded in 1843 by his grandfather, and married twice, decides to give it all up and disappears with quite a large sum of money. He starts a new life in Marseilles with a girl called Julie, who is a cabaret artiste. After he has his money stolen, Julie gets him a job in a rather shabby restaurant checking the orders. By chance he encounters again his first wife, Thérèse, who is companion to a flamboyant middle-aged woman known as 'The Empress'. His wife has become a cocaine addict. Norbert decides to help her and also makes a decision about the future course of his own life.

Comments: One of Simenon's most impressive studies of the flight syndrome. Unpredictable and utterly compelling. 5/5

46) The First-Born

(*L'aîné des Ferchaux*, 1945). Reynal, 1947. Translated as *Magnet Of Doom* (Routledge, 1948; Pan, 1956).

Plot: Dieudonné Ferchaux sets off in the company of his secretary, Michel Maudet, on a voyage from Paris to Panama. The old man is being sought by the police for the murder of three of the natives. He has also abandoned his wife. The two men do not trust each other and decide to separate. But Maudet is planning to rob his boss, and violence ensues.

Comments: According to Simenon this novel was inspired by a real event. 3/5

47) The Couple From Poitiers

(*Les noces de Poitiers*, 1946). Hamilton, 1985; Harcourt, USA, 1986.

Plot: Twenty-year-old Gérard Auvinet marries Linette, who is already pregnant. They leave Poitiers and go to Paris where they experience many disappointments. When Linette gives birth to a girl, Gérard has to take up a job in the provinces.

Comments: The couple face a choice between risking tragedy and accepting a dull but safe existence. 3/5

48) Three Beds In Manhattan

(*Trois chambres à Manhattan*, 1946). Doubleday, USA, 1964; Hamilton, 1976; with two other novels in *Maigret And The Ghost* (Penguin 4676, 1982).

Plot: An actor, François Combe, who was famous in France, has been living in New York for the past six months He is trying to forget a scandal he was involved in. One day he meets a woman called Kay in a bar. She is a divorcee and also just hangs around in bars. They spend the night together and then find it difficult to separate.

Comments: One of the rare novels by Simenon that have an upbeat ending. It appears that the events are based closely on the meeting between Simenon and Denyse Ouimet. 5/5

49) Act Of Passion

(*Lettre à mon juge*, 1947). Routledge Kegan Paul, 1953; Penguin 2245, 1965.

Plot: Charles Alavoine, a medical doctor, has killed his mistress, Martine, and writes a letter to his examining magistrate, whose duty is to collect testimonies and evidence but who does not prosecute or defend him in his trial. The novel consists entirely of this letter, in which Alavoine attempts to understand his own violent act. He reviews his life, from his childhood in the Vendée, through the experience of his father's death from alcoholism, being cared for by an over-protective mother, suffering the death of his first wife, and marrying the dominant Armande. He then makes the acquaintance of Martine, but becomes jealous of the eventful life she has led. How he comes to murder her is the crux of the whole novel.

Comments: As a letter the novel is written in the first person. Simenon manages not only to make the narration utterly convincing but also conjures up the presence of the other major characters with haunting precision, including the examining magistrate himself. Comparisons have been made with the writings of Camus, and many critics regard it as Simenon's one indisputable masterpiece. 5/5

50) The Ostenders

(*Le clan des ostendais*, 1947). In *The House By The Canal* (Routledge Kegan Paul, 1952).

Plot: Fleeing from the Germans in May 1940, a Flemish master fisherman sets off with his family and sailors on board five trawlers. They eventually seek refuge in La Rochelle, but when the occupying troops arrive, the local French inhabitants are not too happy with the situation. Then three of the boats are destroyed by mines.

Comments: An intriguing novel for what it reveals of Simenon's wartime experiences. He was officially in charge of organising accommodation for Belgian refugees in the very area where the novel is situated. 3/5

51) The Fate Of The Malous

(*Le destin des Malous*, 1947). Hamilton, 1962; Penguin 2356, 1966.

Plot: Eugène Malou, a property developer, commits suicide by shooting himself in the head. The shadow of this event hangs over the family for a long time. The youngest son, Alain, seeks to discover what his father was really like.

Comments: A moving story of Alain's journey of discovery, not only about his father but also of himself. 5/5

52) The Stowaway

(*Le passager clandestin*, 1947). Hamilton, 1957.

Plot: A certain Major Owen discovers a woman stowaway on board a cargo ship bound for Tahiti. They both have the same goal in mind: to find the heir of a wealthy movie mogul.

Comments: Simenon returning to the exotic world of the popular novel. 2/5

52) The Reckoning

(*Le bilan Malétras*, 1948). Hamilton, 1984; Harcourt, 1984.

Plot: A wealthy retired retailer, Jules Malétras, has got married again to Hermine de Dodeville. But he also keeps Lulu, a former servant, as his mistress. One evening when she refuses to yield to his desires he strangles her without intending to. With the help of one of the young woman's friends he gets rid of the body, and decides not to give himself up to the police. Eventually he comes to ponder over the way his whole life has gone.

Comments: There is no really intricate plot in this novel. The focus is on making an assessment of a life. The word 'bilan' in the French title has associations with 'balance sheet' and is therefore particularly apt for a review of a shopkeeper's life. 3/5

53) The Snow Was Black

(*La neige était sale*, 1948). Prentice, 1950. Translated as *The Stain On The Snow* (Routledge Kegan Paul, 1953; Penguin 2178, 1964).

Plot: Frank Friedmeier lives with his mother, the manageress of a brothel, in an unnamed European town during the occupation in the Second World War. Just for the pleasure of it he stabs a non-commissioned officer to death and steals his revolver. Soon he commits another murder. He also wins the affections of Sissy, the daughter of his neighbour, but promptly passes her on to someone else. He is arrested by the occupying forces and undergoes a remarkable transformation.

Comments: One of the most harrowing of Simenon's novels, concerning a most unsympathetic central character, but which holds the reader's attention throughout. André Gide described it in a letter to Simenon as a 'remarkable' book. 5/5

54) Pedigree

(*Pedigree*, 1948). Hamilton, 1962; Penguin 2252, 1965.

Plot: This is the most autobiographical of Simenon's novels, though the author himself did not like it described thus. It tells the story of the childhood in Liège of Roger Mamelin, from his birth in 1903, the same year as Simenon, to the end of the First World War. The novel evokes very vividly the experiences of growing up and all the sights and sounds of the city of Liège. Several characters can be recognised as portraits of Simenon's family. Many critics have felt that this work provides the key to understanding Simenon.

Comments: In his preface to the novel Simenon stresses that it was written in a completely different way to his other works, and recognizes that it is completely unique in his output. He also explains how it was written at the encouragement of André Gide. Above all, while recognizing that the central character has much in common with himself as he was as a child, he still wishes it to be considered a novel: '…I would not even wish the label of autobiographical novel to be attached to it.' To make the distinction clear he adds: '…in my novel, everything is true while nothing is accurate.' 5/5

55) The Bottom Of The Bottle

(*Le fond de la bouteille*, 1949). In *Tidal Wave* (Doubleday, USA, 1954; Hamilton, 1977).

Plot: Set in Arizona, this novel tells of a respectable lawyer, P.M. Ashbridge, who encounters his brother Donald, who has just escaped from prison. He takes him in and conceals his true identity from his family and friends, eventually helping him to escape across the frontier. But the story ends tragically for the lawyer.

Comments: The fascination of the novel is in the relationship of the two brothers who have lived utterly different lives. 4/5

56) The Hatter's Ghosts

(*Les phantômes du chapelier*, 1949). Included in *The Judge And The Hatter* (Hamilton, 1956); Penguin 1456, 1960; translated as *The Hatter's Phantoms* (Harcourt, USA, 1976).

Plot: An apparently respectable hat-maker in La Rochelle, M. Labbé, is gradually revealed to be a serial murderer, having killed six women. There is no apparent link between the killings, though one becomes obvious as the novel progresses. Labbé's neighbour, the tailor Kachoudas, becomes convinced that the hatter is indeed the murderer, and stalks his neighbour, not daring to take any action. Labbé writes confident and taunting letters to the local newspaper. He wants people to understand that the murders are necessary, and indeed the reader discovers that there is a twisted logic to them. But the hatter begins to lose control of his well-ordered world, and becomes paranoid (the ghosts are really other people as he sees them).

Comment: A short but utterly compelling novel, the kind it is really difficult to put down. Though written in the third person, everything is told from the point of view of the hatter. One finishes the novel with the feeling that one has not just read about but has experienced directly the mind of a deranged man. The atmosphere in the backstreets and cafés of La Rochelle is also hauntingly real. 5/5

57) Four Days In A Lifetime

(*Les quatre jours du pauvre homme*, 1949). In *Satan's Children* (Prentice, USA, 1953); Hamilton, 1977; with two other novels in *Maigret In Exile* (Penguin 5160, 1983).

Plot: This novel tells the story, in two parts, of the general decline of François Lecoin, from being unemployed to getting involved in a blackmailing racket.

Comments: A novel with no gleam of hope: a failed life that ends in tragedy. 4/5

58) The Burial Of Monsieur Bouvet

(*L'enterrement de Monsieur Bouvet*, 1950). In *Destinations* (Doubleday, USA, 1955); translated as *Inquest on Bouvet* (Hamilton, 1958; Penguin 1679, 1962).

Plot: An elderly man suddenly falls down dead on the banks of the Seine, witnessed by many people. And one man takes a photograph. It appears the man has no family, but the photograph appears in the press and his wife and daughter appear on the scene. It seems that he had lived under various different identities, and had led a very eventful life. The burial is delayed until as much can be discovered about him as possible.

Comments: Simenon at his most subtle and perceptive. A moving story of selfish interest and simple human love. The final sequence is especially well written, with telling circumstantial detail. 5/5

59) The Heart Of A Man

(*Les volets verts*, 1950). Prentice, USA, 1951; in *A Sense Of Guilt* (Hamilton, 1955); Four Square, 1958; in *The Second Simenon Omnibus* (Hamilton, 1974).

Plot: Emile Maugin, is a famous actor of both stage and screen, and has lived life to the full, not only working hard but also drinking and having countless lovers. He is cynical and appears distant to many, but after a strong warning from his heart specialist, he reviews his life and finds he feels an intense sense of guilt that he cannot fathom. He continues to live life to the full, but questions himself and wonders when the moment of death will come.

Comments: A powerful and riveting novel, with many insights into ways in which actors realize character. There are many parallels with the psychology of the writer. It also has something distinctively Kafkaesque in the imaginary 'trial' sequences, and especially in the final stages of the actor's life. It is a pity that the English translations of the original title have distracted attention from the mysterious symbol of 'the green shutters', which haunts the novel and is central to an understanding of it. 5/5

60) Aunt Jeanne

(*Tante Jeanne*, 1950). Routledge Kegan Paul, 1953; Harcourt, USA, 1983.

Plot: An old woman returns to her home village near Poitiers after a forty year absence. Instead of the warm welcome she expected she discovers that her brother has committed suicide and her sister-in-law has become an alcoholic. She endeavours to hold the family together for the sake of the children.

Comments: Another example of a dysfunctional family, with an attempted redemption. 4/5

61) The Girl In His Past

(*Le temps d'Anaïs*, 1951). Prentice, USA, 1952; Hamilton, 1976.

Plot: Albert Bauche has been married to Fernande for five years. He kills his rival Nicholas, unaware that his wife was the man's mistress and had used her influence to get him his job.

Comments: Another novel on the theme of a man trying to escape from an unsatisfying life. The reader gains an understanding of the criminal through an account of his past life. 3/5

62) A New Lease Of Life

(*Une vie comme neuve*, 1951). Hamilton, 1963; Penguin 2388, 1966. Translated as *A New Lease On Life* (Doubleday, USA, 1963).

Plot: An unmarried thirty-nine year-old accountant, Maurice Dudon, steals money from his boss to visit a certain Madame Germaine. One day he is knocked down in a road accident, and this changes his life. He attempts to make a completely new start, but the past soon catches up with him.

Comments: Obsessions die hard, and the wheel of fate comes full circle in this novel. 3/5

63) The Girl With A Squint

(*Marie qui louche*, 1951). Hamilton, 1978; Harcourt, USA, 1978.

Plot: The novel follows the lives of two childhood friends who try to escape from their poor backgrounds, and takes place between the years 1922 and 1950. Sylvie is the more reckless of the two and manages to establish a life of reasonable affluence. But Marie leads a quiet and reserved life with a modest job. After losing touch with each other for many years the two friends decide to try living together again.

Comments: A novel that is characteristic of Simenon's interest in opposing two completely different characters. 4/5

64) Belle

(*La mort de Belle*, 1952). In *Violent Ends* (Hamilton, 1954); in *Tidal Wave* (Doubleday, USA, 1954); Panther, 1958; Signet, 1954.

Plot: Spencer Ashby, a history teacher in a market town in the USA, is accused of murdering a young girl who has been staying with him and his wife. He feels increasingly humiliated by the endless police interrogations and by his dismissal from the college. He begins to behave more and more like a guilty man, although he is in fact innocent. Completely demoralized he begins to do things that are out of character, and eventually lives up to the suspicions that people have of him.

Comments: A fascinating novel for its revelation of the potential criminal in all of us. 5/5

65) The Brothers Rico

(*Les frères Rico*, 1952). In *Violent Ends* (Hamilton, 1954); in *Tidal Wave* (Doubleday, USA, 1954); Four Square, 1957.

Plot: The novel focuses on the three Rico brothers who are members of the family mafia organization, and who get involved in settling scores in a ruthless spiral of violence.

Comments: An atypical novel, for its preoccupation entirely with the mafia, but it became well known through the film version in 1958. 5/5

66) The Magician

(*Antoine et Julie*, 1953). In *The Magician And The Widow* (Doubleday, USA, 1955); Hamilton, 1974; in *The Twelfth Simenon Omnibus* (Penguin 4431, 1977).

Plot: Antoine, a conjuror, and Julie are married. But Antoine is addicted to alcohol. One evening, while he is out drinking, Julie has a sudden attack of angina. But it takes a further attack to disturb his conscience.

Comments: It has been noted that the effects of alcohol on a relationship was a theme close to Simenon's heart. 4/5

67) The Iron Staircase

(*Lescalier de fer*, 1953). Hamilton,1963; Penguin 2590, 1967; Harcourt, USA, 1977; also with another novel in *The Iron Staircase And The Train* (Penguin 8140, 1987).

Plot: Etienne Lomel discovers that his wife poisoned her first husband and is also trying to get rid of him by putting arsenic in his food. He subsequently discovers that she also has a young lover. For him there is only one way to resolve the situation.

Comments: A classic, not particularly original plot, but handled with the usual Simenon subtlety.3/5

68) Red Lights

(*Feux rouges*, 1953). In *Danger Ahead* (Hamilton, 1955); Arrow, 1959; White Lion, 1975; No Exit, 2003; also translated as *The Hitchhiker* (in *Destinations*, Doubleday,1955; Signet, 1957; and in *An American Omnibus*, Harcourt, USA, 1967).

Plot: Steve is jealous of his wife'zs professional success and seeks solace in drink. They have an argument while driving and his wife decides to continue the journey alone. However she is viciously attacked and raped by a stranger. This experience brings the couple closer together again.

Comments: The ending, with its predominantly optimistic tone, makes it a rarity among Simenon novels.4/5

69) The Fugitive

(*Crime impuni*, 1954). Doubleday, USA, 1955. Translated as *Account Unsettled* (Hamilton, 1962; Penguin 2316, 1966).

Plot: The novel starts in the 20s in Liège with a young Polish student, Elie, who is in love with Louise, but who cannot stand the attentions paid her by the rich and handsome young Romanian, Michel. One foggy night Elie guns Michel down. The scene then changes to twenty-five years later in Arizona, when Elie meets again the man he thought he had killed.

Comments: Of special interest because of the sharp contrasts between the characters of the two men, between two different periods and two completely different countries. 3/5

70) The Watchmaker Of Everton

(*L'horloger d'Everton*, 1954). In *Danger Ahead* (Hamilton, 1955); Arrow, 1959. Translated as *The Watchmaker* in *The Witnesses And The Watchmaker* (Doubleday, USA, 1956); this translation reissued as *The Clockmaker* (Harvest, 1977).

Plot: Dave Galloway, a watchmaker in a village in the state of New York, is devoted to his son Ben since his wife left him. One night Ben does not come home. Shortly after, Dave is shocked to learn that his son, who is sixteen, is being sought by the police for murder. When his son is imprisoned he decides to help him, but Ben is indifferent to his interest and does not want to see his father. Despite the pain his son's attitude causes him, Dave identifies with his son and tries to understand him.

Comments: One of Simenon's most moving novels about the relationship between father and son. Written with great sensitivity. 5/5

71) Big Bob

(*Le grand Bob*, 1954). Hamilton, 1969; in *The Fifth Simenon Omnibus* (Penguin 3432, 1972); Harcourt, USA, 1981.

Plot: A doctor tries to understand the death of a friend, who seemed so happy and full of life. It is not clear at first whether the death was an accident or suicide.

Comments: A poignant story with a tragic ending. 5/5

72) The Witnesses

(*Les témoins*, 1955). In *The Judge And The Hatter* (Hamilton, 1956); in *The Witnesses And The Watchmaker* (Doubleday, USA, 1956); Four Square, 1958.

Plot: A magistrate at the court of assizes, Xavier Lhomond, has the job of investigating the soundness of the evidence against a man appearing before the court, and notices similarities with his own situation. He has a wife with cardiac problems, which forces him to be absent too often.

Comments: A subtle analysis of responsibility and guilt. 4/5

73) The Accomplices

(*Les complices*, 1956). In *The Blue Room And The Accomplices* (Harcourt, USA, 1964); Signet, 1965; Hamilton, 1966; in *The Second Simenon Omnibus* (Penguin 3185, 1970).

Plot: Joseph Lambert is responsible for a bad road accident, in which several children are killed. He is accompanied by his secretary, Edmonde, who is also his lover, when the accident happens and he decides to drive off and not give himself up to the police. He can be certain of Edmonde's silence, and is not particularly concerned at first, but gradually he becomes filled with remorse, and feels that there can be only one solution.

Comments: An utterly convincing study of a man who becomes racked by remorse. 5/5

74) In Case Of Emergency

(*En cas de malheur*, 1956). Doubleday, USA, 1958; Hamilton, 1960; Penguin 2254, 1965; in *In Case Of Emergency And The Little Saint* (Penguin 8138, 1986).

Plot: Lucien Gobillot, is a prominent defence lawyer who married the widow of his former boss, and moves in the best social circles. One day a young prostitute, Yvette, asks him to defend her and also offers herself to him. He fights off her advances at first but eventually gives in. He provides Yvette with her own apartment, but then learns that a spurned lover is threatening her. And tragedy indeed ensues.

Comments: The novel is written in the form of a diary, a kind of secret report on himself, or dossier, as Lambert calls it. This means that the reader has the illusion of experiencing the events as they happen. One of the themes of the novel is that there are still so many unanswerable questions about the motivations of the self. A justly famous book, which was also made into a successful film. 5/5

75) The Little Man From Archangel

(*Le petit homme d'Arkhangelsk*, 1956). Hamilton, 1957; Penguin 1854, 1964; in *A Simenon Omnibus* (Hamilton, 1965); in *The Little Man From Archangel And Monsieur Monde Vanishes* (Penguin 8139, 1986).

Plot: Jonas Milk, a timid, forty year-old bookseller and a Russian Jew, is living happily with his young wife, Gina, when one day she disappears. It seems likely that the young woman has gone off with a lover, but Jonas does not want to discuss the matter and is suspected of killing her.

Comments: The atmosphere of the provincial town is well evoked. The ending is especially moving. 4/5

76) The Son

(*Le fils*, 1957). Hamilton, 1956; Four Square, 1962.

Plot: On the death of his father, Alain Lefrançois starts telling his own sixteen year-old son the story of his life. He is haunted by a secret that he shared with his father. His father considered himself responsible for the death of Alain's pregnant girlfriend. In writing this confession to his son, he hopes to gain his son's understanding.

Comments: Interesting especially for the study of the relationships between three generations of a family. 4/5

77) The Negro

(*Le nègre*, 1957). Hamilton, 1959; Ace, 1962.

Plot: A Negro's corpse is found one winter's morning by a railway embankment. It is suspected that he fell from the late-night train from Amiens, but Théo, the keeper of a small station nearby, saw the figure of the Negro, in full moonlight, going away from the embankment towards the village. It is obvious therefore that the man met his death by some other means, and only Théo has knowledge of this evidence. The Cadieu brothers seem likely to be implicated in the affair, and Théo sees his chance to change his dreary life once and for all with the help of a little blackmail.

Comments: The critics have been sharply divided about this work, some classing it as a minor work, others as a convincing psychological study of a man desperately trying to escape from a boring life in which he feels inferior to others. 4/5

78) The Premier

(*Le président*, 1958). Hamilton, 1961; Penguin 2064, 1964; in *A Simenon Omnibus* (Hamilton, 1965); in *The Premier And The Train* (Harcourt, USA, 1966).

Plot: A former Premier, retired following an electoral defeat, is writing his memoirs in his cliff-top home in Normandy. He dreams of returning to power through a government crisis. He has one hope: he has a hold over his former secretary, Chalamont, who is said to be forming the next government. Chalamont once betrayed him and the country, and the former Premier still has the man's written confession. Will he do a deal?

Comments: It is unusual for Simenon to set a novel entirely in the world of politics, but his portrait of the ageing statesman desperately wanting to cling onto all the influence he has is very convincing. 4/5

79) Striptease

(*Strip-tease*, 1958). Hamilton, 1959; Penguin 1853; in *The Second Simenon Omnibus*, Hamilton, 1974.

Plot: Célita, a dancer in the Monaco bar in Cannes, is the mistress of the proprietor but covets the situation of his wife, because of her secure position. The arrival of a new dancer, Maud, who proves to have a sensational way of stripping, complicates the situation.

Comments: There are many familiar Simenon themes in the novel, such as fear of mediocrity, a desire to escape from an unfulfilling life and the gradual decline of an individual.3/5

80) Sunday

(*Dimanche*, 1959). Hamilton, 1960; Penguin 2018, 1963; in *A Simenon Omnibus* (Hamilton, 1965); in *Sunday And The Little Man From Archangel* (Harcourt, USA, 1966).

Plot: Émile is married to a domineering older wife. It is her family who own the inn, 'La Bastide', which they run together near Nice. Émile is the chef but feels like a servant. To assert his independence he takes a maid as his mistress, but is still continually humiliated by his wife. Finally he hatches a plot to poison his wife, but reckons without his wife's own ingenuity.

Comments: Although set on one day, the narrative concurrently reveals events from the past. It is a masterly study of a mind obsessed. 5/5

81) The Grandmother

(*La vieille*, 1959). In *The White Horse Inn* (Hamilton, 1980); Harcourt, USA, 1980.

Plot: A grandmother agrees to spend her last years with her granddaughter, a famous parachutist. Being very much alike, however, the two women are soon at loggerheads.

Comments: Unusual among Simenon's works for having two female protagonists. A riveting study of loneliness and the problems of communication. 4/5

82) The Widower

(*Le veuf*, 1959). Hamilton, 1961; Penguin 2253, 1965; in *The Second Simenon Omnibus* (Hamilton, 1974); Harcourt, USA, 1982.

Plot: A forty year-old man tries to understand why his wife has committed suicide alone in a Paris hotel room. Investigating her past he discovers that she was keeping something secret from him.

Comments: The novel deals with the not uncommon habit among Simenon characters of leading a double life. 3/5

83) Teddy Bear

(*L'ours en peluche*, 1960). Hamilton, 1971; Harcourt, USA, 1972; in *The Eighth Simenon Omnibus* (Penguin 3897, 1975).

Plot: A famous gynecologist leads a dull family life, which he attempts to escape from through his relationship with his secretary, Viviane. He also has a brief affair with a woman called Emma, the 'Teddy Bear' of the title, but when she is rejected by the gynecologist's circle she commits suicide. He becomes dominated by a sense of responsibility for Emma's death, and his despair eventually turns into aggression.

Comments: A sombre and unremitting novel, but compelling to the very end. 5/5

84) Betty

(*Betty*, 1961). Harcourt, USA, 1975; Hamilton, 1975; in *The Fourteenth Simenon Omnibus* (Penguin 4675, 1979).

Plot: A young woman of twenty-eight, Betty Etamble, is forced to leave her husband by her in-laws, who consider her conduct to be scandalous. She escapes into a sleazy world of drug addicts and drunks, and finally takes refuge in a hotel with a doctor's widow called Laure Lavancher, in whom she confides everything. Laure's decision to help Betty has a tragic outcome.

Comments: A haunting story turned into a successful film by Claude Chabrol. 5/5

85) The Train

(*Le train*, 1961). Hamilton, 1964; in *The Premier And The Train* (Harcourt, USA, 1966); Penguin 2566, 1967; in *The Iron Staircase And The Train* (Penguin 8140, 1987).

Plot: Marcel Féron flees the German invasion in the spring of 1940 with his pregnant wife and four year-old daughter. He becomes separated from his family while being evacuated by train. He meets a young Jewish girl, Anna, and they become lovers. When the train arrives in La Rochelle, Marcel and Anna meet again in a camp, but Marcel soon learns that his wife is not far away and has given birth. He decides to go back to his wife. But later, when he and his family are together again in the Ardennes, the Jewish girl turns up again, needing his help.

Comments: The setting of the novel is utterly convincing and no doubt owes much to Simenon's own experiences of helping refugees during the war. 4/5

86) The Door

(*La porte*, 1962). Hamilton,1964; Penguin 2680,1968.

Plot: Bernard, a war invalid, who has lost his hands, lives with his wife Nelly in Paris. One day he finds his wife in the arms of their neighbour, a young handicapped man. This, not unnaturally, induces a severe emotional crisis in Bernard.

Comments: Simenon works do not come much bleaker than this. 3/5

87) The Others

(*Les autres*, 1962). Hamilton, 1975; in *The Thirteenth Simenon Omnibus* (Penguin 4511, 1978); also translated as *The House On Quai Notre Dame* (Harcourt, USA, 1975).

Plot: A forty year-old art teacher, Blaise Huet, is writing a journal. The death of an uncle and the unexpected return of a cousin lead him to reflect on his life.

Comments: This is quite a short novel, but it manages to reflect very well the infighting that goes on within a provincial family. 4/5

88) The Patient

(*Les anneaux de Bicêtre*, 1963). Hamilton, 1963; Penguin 2814, 1968; also translated as *The Bells Of Bicêtre* (Harcourt, USA, 1964; Signet, 1965).

Plot: A wealthy press mogul, René Maugras, is in the hospital at Bicêtre, after becoming unwell in a restaurant. He is paralysed but gradually regains contact with the world around him, and reviews his life, his successes and failures, and also his marriage to Lina, who has long been an alcoholic.

Comments: A familiar theme of a man in crisis reviewing his life, but this one has an upbeat quality that makes it enjoyable. 3/5

89) The Blue Room

(*La chambre bleue*, 1964). In *The Blue Room And The Accomplices* (Harcourt, USA, 1964); Hamilton, 1965; Signet, 1965; Penguin 2789, 1968; in the series 'Crime Masterworks,' Orion, 2002.

Plot: Tony and Andrée knew each other as children, and when they discover each other again in later years they become lovers. But they are both already married, and when Andrée's husband almost discovers them together one day, Tony decides it would be best for them to part, but Andrée is determined that their relationship should continue, at whatever cost.

Comments: An intense, very memorable novel, providing a haunting analysis of obsessive love. It also reflects Simenon's concern, which is expressed in several of the Maigret novels, about the difficulties in French law for a defendant to prove his or her innocence. 5/5

90) The Man With The Little Dog

(*L'homme au petit chien*, 1964). Hamilton, 1965; and in *The Fourth Simenon Omnibus* (Penguin 3337, 1971).

Plot: Félix Allart has come out of prison and leads a quiet life with the company of his little dog, expecting that he will die soon, as his doctor has predicted. He writes down an account of his life in a school exercise book, including a report on how he worked as a clerk, made some success of himself, and finally murdered his wife's lover.

Comments: For most readers the ending of this novel is a shock, and at the same time beautifully ironic. 3/5

91) The Little Saint

(*Le petit saint*, 1965). Harcourt, USA, 1965; Hamilton, 1966; in *The Fourth Simenon Omnibus* (Penguin 3337, 1971); in *In Case Of Emergency And The Little Saint* (Penguin 8138, 1986).

Plot: The novel traces the development of a painter, Louis Cuchas, and his art, and reveals how he remained faithful to his childhood experiences.

Comments: The novel is rare amongst Simenon's works in showing how a man raises himself above his environment and attains some greatness. 5/5

92) The Venice Train

(*Le train de Venise*, 1965). Hamilton, 1974; Harcourt, USA, 1974; in *The Eleventh Simenon Omnibus* (Penguin 4248, 1977).

Plot: Justin Calmar is asked by a stranger on board a train from Venice to deliver a briefcase to an address in Lausanne. He agrees, only to find that he is holding a fortune in currency, but has a corpse on his hands. He decides to keep the money but not tell his wife and family about it. His reward is only lies and fear.

Comments: The strength of the novel lies in its analysis of anxiety. 4/5

93) The Confessional

(*Le confessional*, 1966). Hamilton, 1967; Harcourt, USA, 1968; in *The Seventh Simenon Omnibus* (Penguin 3838, 1974).

Plot: The story focuses on the completely dysfunctional family of a dentist. The constant disagreements between the parents cause great distress to the schoolboy son, André, who seeks comfort in the arms of a girl from a more stable background.

Comments: It has been claimed that the novel reflects many of the personal problems in Simenon's own family. 3/5

94) The Old Man Dies

(*La mort d'Auguste*, 1966). Harcourt, USA, 1967; Hamilton, 1968; in *The Third Simenon Omnibus* (Penguin 3324, 1971).

Plot: When Auguste, the owner of a restaurant in Les Halles, Paris, dies, his three sons fight each other for their inheritance. A shock is in store for them.

Comments: A novel about a family dominated by selfish avarice. 3/5

95) The Cat

(*Le chat*, 1967). Harcourt, 1967; Hamilton, 1972; in *The Ninth Simenon Omnibus* (Penguin 3980, 1976).

Plot: After losing their spouses, Marguerite and Emile marry each other out of the need to avoid loneliness. But they begin to loathe each other. One day Emile's cat is poisoned and, suspecting Marguerite of having done it, Emile refuses to speak to her. From then on they only communicate by notes, though they discover that they cannot actually bring themselves to separate. The future is indeed bleak.

Comments: A very disturbing book to read, providing little comfort. Somehow a relationship survives on purely negative feelings. The couple is held together by their own emptiness. Brilliantly honest about a human relationship at its worst. Jean Gabin and Simone Signoret have interpreted the characters convincingly in the film version. 5/5

96) The Neighbours

(*Le déménagement*, 1967). Hamilton, 1968; in *The First Simenon Omnibus* (Penguin 3184, 1970); also translated as *The Move* (Harcourt, USA, 1968).

Plot: The director of a Paris travel agency, Emile Jovis, leaves his apartment in the Rue des Francs-Bourgeois and moves to a modern apartment in the suburbs. But the walls are very thin, and he overhears the conversations of his new neighbour, who turns out to be the owner of a striptease club in Paris. It is a whole new sleazy world for Emile, and he becomes drawn into the clutches of a gang of crooks.

Comments: The novel is interesting for its contrast between traditional values and an amoral world. 4/5

97) The Prison

(*La prison*, 1968). Hamilton, 1969; Harcourt, USA, 1969; in *The Sixth Simenon Omnibus* (Penguin 3542, 1972).

Plot: The wife of the director of a weekly magazine has killed her own sister. The director is mystified and tries to find out why she did it. The two sisters never liked each other, but there is something in their past which fired their common hatred.

Comments: The past rears its ugly head to rob the present of meaning and purpose. Yet another Simenon novel in which the central character discovers the pointlessness of his own existence. 3/5

98) The Man On The Bench In The Barn

(*La main*, 1968). Hamilton, 1970; Harcourt, USA, 1969; in *The Tenth Simenon Omnibus* (Penguin 3668, 1976).

Plot: Two couples returning from a reception in the snowbound district of Connecticut, America, have to abandon their car, which gets stuck in snowdrifts. When they arrive at the house of Donald Dodd, it is discovered that one member of the group, Ray, has disappeared. Donald pretends to go off searching for him but in fact hides in the barn. Two days later Ray's body is found, but Donald does not consider himself responsible for his friend's death. Eventually Ray's widow becomes Donald's lover, but the affair ends tragically.

Comments: A novel written in the first person, a mode that Simenon handled with mastery. It is another attempt of a murderer to understand his own behaviour. It is also a novel set entirely in America; unlike the others, it was written many years after Simenon's actual stay there. 3/5

99) November

(*Novembre*, 1969). Hamilton, 1970; Harcourt, USA, 1970; in *The Fifth Simenon Omnibus* (Penguin 3432, 1972).

Plot: The usual dismal weather in November reflects the mood in the Le Cloanec family. Each member of the family lives in his or her own world: the mother is a drunkard, the father is sullenly absorbed in his work, and the children are struggling with their adolescent crises. A pretty young Spanish maid, Manuella, disturbs the household by dispensing her favours to the son, and eventually to the father. But one day Manuella disappears.

Comments: The novel is about a family, which was heading for disaster one way or the other. Manuela happens to be the catalyst. Only one character, the daughter Laure, manages to rise above it all. She is also the narrator. 3/5

100) The Rich Man

(*Le riche homme*, 1970). Hamilton, 1971; Harcourt, USA, 1971; in *The Sixth Simenon Omnibus* (Penguin 3542, 1972).

Plot: Victor Lecoin, a prosperous mussel-cultivator, lives in Marsilly and is envied by his neighbours as 'the rich man'. He is married to Jeanne, but indulges himself in various amorous adventures, which everybody knows about. He falls in a big way for their new maid Alice, but then Alice is found murdered.

Comments: A central theme is the short-lived nature of happiness. 3/5

101) The Disappearance Of Odile

(*La disparition d'Odile*, 1971). Hamilton, 1972; Harcourt, USA, 1972; in *The Ninth Simenon Omnibus* (Penguin 3980, 1976).

Plot: An eighteen year-old girl, Odile Pointet, decides to leave her family house in Lausanne for Paris. In a letter to her brother she tells him she is contemplating suicide. He promptly sets out to find her. She meets up with a young medical student who saves her from a suicide attempt by using a tourniquet, and gives her new hope.

Comments: This is a rare example of Simenon allowing hope to be born in the midst of despair. All the more ironic, when one considers that his own daughter, Marie-Jo, would commit suicide only two years later. 4/5

102) The Glass Cage

(*La cage de verre*, 1971). Hamilton, 1973; Harcourt, USA, 1978; in *The Tenth Simenon Omnibus* (Penguin 3668, 1976).

Plot: Emile Virieu, forty-four years old, is a corrector in a printing works and works in an office that is a kind of glass cage, and which gives him a certain sense of security. But suddenly his world is turned upside down by his brother-in-law's suicide. Emile becomes emotionally unstable and cannot control his feelings, which has lethal effects.

Comments: The novel traces the slow but sure progress from repression of all feelings to pathological behaviour. 4/5

103) The Innocents

(*Les innocents*, 1972). Hamilton, 1973; Harcourt, USA, 1974; in *The Eleventh Simenon Omnibus* (Penguin 4248, 1977).

Plot: Georges Célerin, a jeweller, has been living an apparently normal family life, but after his wife is accidentally run over and killed in the Rue Washington, it is revealed that she had been deceiving him for eighteen years, and with someone he knew very well.

Comments: This last of the 'romans durs' undertakes no new departures thematically, and in fact returns to a favourite Simenon interest: the effect on others of the revelation that someone has been leading a double life. 5/5

5. Simenon On Film

The listings are divided into films based on Maigret novels and those based on 'romans durs', and each list is chronological by the year in which the films were first released. The original title is indicated first (in its original language, where possible) and the country of origin, together with the year of release. This is followed by the title of the first English translation of the original work on which the film is based, with a reference to the more detailed entries in the relevant checklists (M+number for the Maigret novels, and RD+number for the 'romans durs'). The subsequent headings depend on the information available for each film, but include as a rule: Director, Adaptation (which includes screenplay and dialogue), and Main Actors (some well-known French actors are known by their family names only). Further information and comments are added where relevant. Only those films for which information can be verified through reliable sources have been included. The listings are therefore not exhaustive. One film has been deliberately omitted, because it only contains a short sketch based on the Maigret short story 'The Evidence Of The Altar Boy', amongst other sketches. The title of the film is *Brelan d'As*, directed by Henri Verneuil, with Michel Simon as Maigret, and released in 1952.

Maigret On Film

1) La nuit du carrefour

France, 1932. (*The Crossroads Murder*, M6.) *Director*: Jean Renoir. *Adaptation*: Jean Renoir and Georges Simenon.

Main Actors: Pierre Renoir (Maigret), Winna Winfried, Georges Koudria, Georges Terof, Dignimont, Lucie Vallat.

2) Le chien jaune

France, 1932. (*A Face For A Clue*, M4.) *Director*: Jean Tarride. *Adaptation*: Jean Tarride and Georges Simenon.

Main Actors: Abel Tarride (Maigret), Rosine Derean, Jane Lory, Rolla Norman, Anthony Gildès, Robert Le Vigan.

3) La tête d'un homme

France, 1933. (*A Battle Of Nerves*, M9.) *Director*: Julian Duvivier. *Adaptation*: Loius Delaprée, Julien Duvivier and Pierre Caldmann.

Main Actors: Harry Baur (Maigret), Valéry Inkijinoff, Gina Manès, Lina Noro, Gaston Jacquet, Alexandre Rignault.

Comments: Inkijinoff and Simenon themselves had worked on an adaptation of the novel, which Simenon thought of producing himself, but this was not used by Duvivier.

4) Picpus

France, 1943. (*To Any Lengths*, M23.) *Director*: Richard Pottier. *Adaptation*:
Jean-Paul le Chanois.

Main Actors: Albert Préjean (Maigret), Jean Tissier, Delmont, Juliette Faber,
Guillaume de Sax, Noël Roquevert.

5) Cécile est morte

France, 1944. (*Maigret And The Spinster*, M20.) *Director*: Maurice Tourneur.
Adaptation: Jean-Paul le Chanois and Michel Duran.

Main Actors: Albert Préjean (Maigret), Santa Relli, Germaine Kerjean, Luce
Fabiole, Liliane Maigné, Gabriello, André Reybaz.

6) Les caves du Majestic

France, 1945. (*Maigret And The Hotel Majestic*, M21.) *Director*: Richard Pot-
tier. *Adaptation*: Charles Spaak.

Main Actors: Albert Préjean (Maigret), Gabriello, Suzy Prim, Jean Marchat,
Denise Grey, Jacques Baumer, René Génin, Florelle.

7) The Man On The Eiffel Tower

USA, 1949. (*A Battle Of Nerves*, M9.) *Director*: Burgess Meredith. *Adaptation*:
Harry Brown and John Cortez.

Main Actors: Charles Laughton (Maigret), Franchot Tone, Burgess Meredith,
Robert Hutton, Jean Wallace, Patricia Roc, Belita, George Thorpe, William
Phipps, William Cottrell, Chaz Chase, Wilfrid Hyde-White, Howard Vernon.

8) Maigret dirige l'enquête

United Kingdom (?), 1956. (Based on various works. See comment below.)
Director: Stany Cordier. *Adaptation*: ?

Main Actors: Maurice Manson (Maigret), Svetlana Pitoëff, Peter Walker, Michel
André, André Tabet.

Comments: One of the mysteries of cinematic history. It is a film that is rarely
shown, and one critic who viewed it in 1979 was not able to come to any firm
conclusions about it. It seems to be a British film, but filmed in Paris for the
exterior shots. The actor, named in the credits as Maurice Manson, who plays
Maigret, looks uncannily like Georges Simenon! Generally the film is consid-
ered disastrous, but has novelty value. It consists of several sketches based
loosely on three Maigret works: *Maigret And The Spinster*, *Death Of A
Nobody*, and *Maigret And The Burglar's Wife*.

9) Maigret tend un piège

France, 1958. (*Maigret Sets A Trap*, M52.) *Director*: Jean Delannoy. *Adaptation*: Rodolphe-Marie Arlaud, Michel Audiard and Jean Delannoy.
Main Actors: Jean Gabin (Maigret), Annie Girardot, Jean Desailly, Jeanne Boitel, Gérard Séty, Lucienne Bogaërt, Jean Debucourt, Olivier Hussenot, Lino Ventura.

10) Maigret et l'affaire Saint-Fiacre

France, 1959. (*L'Affaire Saint-Fiacre*, M13.) *Director*: Jean Delannoy. *Adaptation*: Rodolphe-Marie Arlaud, Jean Delannoy and Michel Audiard.
Main Actors: Jean Gabin (Maigret), Valentine Tessier, Michel Auclair, Michel Vitold, Robert Hirsch, Paul Frankeur, Jacques Morel, Armande Navarre.

11) Maigret voit rouge

France, 1963. (*Inspector Maigret And The Killers*, M43.) *Director*: Gilles Grangier. *Adaptation*: Jacques Robert and Gilles Grangier.
Main Actors: Jean Gabin (Maigret), Françoise Fabian, Vittorio Sanipoli, Paul Carpenter, Ricky Cooper, Brad Harris, Michel Constantin, Paul Frankeur, Harry Max, Guy Decomble.

12) Maigret und sein größter Fall

Federal Republic of Germany, 1966. (*At The 'Gai Moulin'*, M10.) *Director*: Alfred Weidemann. *Adaptation*: Herbert Reinecker.
Main Actors: Heinz Rühmann (Maigret), Françoise Prévost, Günther Stoll, Günter Strack, Gerd Vespermann, Eddi Arent, Günther Ungeheuer, Alexander Kerst, Ulli Lommel.

13) Maigret a Pigalle

Italy, 1967. (*Maigret In Montmartre*, M40.) *Director*: Mario Landi. *Adaptation*: Sergio Amidei, Mario Landi, and Georges and André Tabet.
Main Actors: Gino Cervi (Maigret), Lila Kedrova, Raymond Pellegrin, Alfred Adam, Christian Barbier, Josée Greci, Daviel Ollier, Enzo Cerusico.
Comments: This is a film version made as a spin-off from the long-running Italian TV series starring Gino Cervi. The first episode was also called *Maigret a Pigalle* and broadcast in 1962. 36 episodes were planned for the series.

'Romans Durs' On Film

1) Dernier refuge

France, 1940. (*The Lodger*, RD10.) *Director*: Jacques Constant. *Adaptation*: Jacques Constant and André-Paul Antoine.

Main Actors: Mireille Balin, Georges Rigaud, Marie Glory, Dalio, Saturnin Fabre, Mila Parely, Jean Tissier, Argentin, Roger Blin.

Comments: This film is no longer available. Filming was apparently started in August, 1939 at the Studios Saint-Maurice, but was interrupted after three weeks because of the declaration of war on 3rd September. It continued eventually and the production was finished in April, 1940. The original negatives of the film were destroyed during a laboratory fire.

2) Annette et la dame blonde

France, 1942. (Based on a short story not translated into English, but meaning 'Annette And The Blonde Woman'. Published in a collection with the title *La rue aux trois poussins*, 1963.) *Director*: Jean Dréville. *Adaptation:* Henri Decoin and Duran.

Main Actors: Louise Carletti, Henri Garat, Georges Rollin, Mona Goya, Simone Valère, Rosine Luguet, Marcelle Rexiane.

3) La maison des sept jeunes filles

France, 1942. (Not translated into English. The original was published by Gallimard in 1941. The literal translation is 'The House Of The Seven Young Girls.') *Director*: Albert Valentin. *Adaptation*: Jacques Viot, Maurice Blondeau and Charles Spaak.

Main Actors: André Brunot, Jean Tissier, Jean Paqué, Jean Rigaux, Marguerite Deval, René Bergeron, Paul Demange. The seven young girls were played by Gaby Andreu, Geneviève Beau, Jacqueline Bouvier, Josette Daydé, Solange Delporte, Marianne Hardy and Primerose Perret.

4) Les inconnus dans la maison

France, 1942. (*The Strangers In The House*, RD33.) *Director*: Henri Decoin. *Adaptation*: Henri-Georges Clouzot.

Main Actors: Raimu, Juliette Faber, Gabrielle Fontan, Jacques Baumer, Héléna Manson, Jean Tissier, Lucien Coëdel.

Comments: Apparently Joseph Losey refused to do a remake in 1963, because of what he described as a disastrous adaptation by George Tabori.

5) Monsieur La Souris

France, 1942. (*Monsieur La Souris*, RD26.) *Director:* Georges Lacombe. *Adaptation*: Marcel Achard.

Main Actors: Raimu, Aimé Clariond, Charles Granval, Micheline Francey, Aimos, Pierre Jourdan, Gilbert Gil, Marie Carlot.

Comments: Under the title *Midnight In Paris* this was apparently the first film based on a Simenon novel to be released in America.

6) Le voyager de la Toussaint

France, 1943. (*Strange Inheritance*, RD38.) *Director:* Louis Daquin. *Adaptation:* Marcel Aymé and Louis Daquin.

Main Actors: Assia Noris, Jules Berry, Gabrielle Dorziat, Guillaume de Sax, Roger Karl, Louis Seigner, Alexandre Rigault.

Comments: Apparently, if the viewer remains alert, it is possible to spot Simone Signoret among the extras.

7) L'homme de Londres

France, 1943. (*Newhaven-Dieppe*, RD9.) *Director:* Henri Decoin. *Adaptation*: Henri Decoin and Charles Exbrayat.

Main Actors: Fernand Ledoux, Jules Berry, Suzy Prim, Hélène Manson, Blanche Montel, Jean Brochard, Mony Damès.

8) Panique

France, 1947. (*Mr. Hire's Engagement*, RD4.) *Director*: Julien Duvivier. *Adaptation*: Charles Spaak and Julien Duvivier.

Main Actors: Michel Simon, Viviane Romance, Paul Bernard, Charles Dorat, Max Dalban, Magdeleine Gidon, Lucas Gridoux.

9) Dernier refuge

France, 1947. (*The Lodger*, RD10.) *Director*: Marc Maurette. *Adaptation*: Marc Maurette and Maurice Griffe.

Main Actors: Raymond Rouleau, Mila Parely, Gisèle Pascal, Jean Max, Marcel Carpentier, Noêl Roquevert, Tramel.

10) Temptation Harbour

Also released as *Newhaven-Dieppe*, and in France as *Le port de la tentation*.

United Kingdom, 1948. (*Newhaven-Dieppe*, RD9.) *Director*: Lance Confort. *Adaptation*: Victor Skutezky, Frederic Gotfurt and Rodney Ackland.

Main Actors: Robert Newton, Simone Simon, William Hartnell, Marcel Dalio, Margaret Barton, Erward Rigby, Joan Hopkins, Charles Victor, Kathleen Harrison, Irene Handl.

11) La Marie du port

France, 1950. (*Chit Of A Girl*, RD27.) *Director*: Marcel Carné. *Adaptation*: Louis Chavance, Marcel Carné and Georges Ribemont.

Main Actors: Jean Gabin, Nicole Courcel, Blanchette Brunoy, Claude Romain, Julien Carette, Jane Marken, Georges Vitray.

Comments: It is reported that the writer Jacques Prévert worked on the design of the film, but this was not officially acknowledged. Rumours went around for several years about the plans for the film. For a long time it was assumed that it would be directed by Pierre Billon, and the artist Maurice de Vlaminck would design the décor. That would have been an interesting choice, as Vlaminck was a close personal friend of Simenon.

12) Midnight Episode

USA, 1950. (*Monsieur La Souris*, RD26.) *Director*: Gordon Parry. *Adaptation*: Rita Barriss, Reeve Taylor, Paul Vincent-Carroll, David Evans and William Templeton.

Main Actors: Stanley Holloway, Leslie Dwyer, Reginald Tate, Meredith Edwards, Wilfred Hyde-White, Joe Shelton, Natasha Parry, Raymond Young, Leslie Perrins, Sebastian Cabot.

13) La vérité sur Bébé Donge

France, 1952. (*The Trial Of Bébé Donge*, RD41.) *Director*: Henri Decoin. *Adaptation*: Maurice Aubergé.

Main Actors: Danielle Darrieux, Jean Gabin, Daniel Lecourtois, Claude Genia, Gabrielle Dorziat, Jacqueline Porel, Jacques Castelot.

14) Le fruit défendu

France, 1952. (*Act Of Passion*, RD49.) *Director*: Henri Verneuil. *Adaptation*: Jacques Companeez, Jean Manse and Henri Verneuil.

Main Actors: Fernandel, Sylvie, Françoise Arnoul, Claude Nollier, Jacques Castelot, Raymond Pellegrin, René Génin.

Comments: It was a brave decision indeed to cast the famous comic actor Fernandel as an obsessed murderer.

15) The Man Who Watched The Trains Go By

USA, 1953. (*The Man Who Watched The Trains Go By*, RD28.) *Director*: Harold French. *Adaptation*: Harold French.

Main Actors: Claude Rains, Marta Toren, Marius Goring, Herbert Lom, Anouk Aimée, Lucie Mannheim, Felix Aylmer, Eric Pohlmann, Ferdy Maine.

Comments: The film is said to have been offered to Joseph Losey but then he was put on the anti-communist blacklist and had to leave Hollywood.

16) La neige était sale

France, 1954. (*The Snow Was Black*, RD53.) *Director*: Luis Saslavsky. *Adaptation*: André Bac, Luis Saslavsky and André Tabet.

Main Actors: Daniel Gélin, Valentine Tessier, Marie Mansart, Daniel Ivernel, Véra Norman, Nadine Basile, Joëlle Bernard, Antoine Balpêtre.

17) A Life In The Balance

USA, 1955. ('A Matter Of Life And Death', also translated as 'Seven Little Crosses In A Notebook' in *Maigret's Christmas*.) *Director*: Harry Horner (with co-director, Rafael Portillo). *Adaptation*: Robert Presnell Jnr and Leo Townsend.

Main Actors: Ricardo Montalban, Anne Bancroft, Lee Marvin, José Parez, Rodolfo Acosta, Carlos Muzquiz, Jorge Trevino.

18) The Bottom Of The Bottle

USA, 1955. (*The Bottom Of The Bottle*, RD55.) *Director*: Henry Hathaway. *Adaptation*: Sidney Boehm.

Main Actors: Van Johnson, Joseph Cotton, Ruth Roman, Jack Carson, Bruce Bennett, Brad Dexter, Peggy Knudsen, Jim Davis.

19) Le sang à la tête

France, 1956. (*Young Cardinaud*, RD40.) *Director*: Gilles Grangier. *Adaptation*: Gilles Grangier and Michel Audiard.

Main Actors: Jean Gabin, Paul Frankeur, Renée Faure, Monique Mélinard, José Quaglio, Claude Sylvain, Georgette Anys.

20) Le passager clandestin

France, 1958. (*The Stowaway*, RD52.) *Director*: Ralph Habib. *Adaptation*: Maurice Aubergé, Ralph Habib and Paul Andréota.

Main Actors: Martine Carol, Karl-Heinz Boehm, Arletty, Serge Reggiani, Roger Livesey, Reginald Lye, Maea Flohr.

Comments: It would appear that this was an international co-production as production is credited to Discifilm and Siver Film in Paris, but also to Southern International, Sydney. The list of actors is also truly international, including, among others, French, German, Italian and British actors.

21) The Brothers Rico

USA, 1958. (*The Brothers Rico*, RD65.) *Director*: Phil Karlson. *Adaptation*: Lewis Maltzer, Ben Perry and Burnet Guffey.

Main Actors: Richard Conte, Dianne Fister, Kathryn Grant, Peter Lamont, Larry Gates, James Darren, Paul Picerni, Argentina Brunetti.

Comments: There was a TV remake in 1972, entitled *The Family Rico*, directed by Paul Wendkos, and starring Ben Gazzara, James Farentino, Jo Van Fleet, Dane Clark and John Morley.

22) En cas de malheur

France, 1958. (*In Case Of Emergency*, RD74.) *Director*: Claude Autant-Lara.
Adaptation: Jean Aurenche and Pierre Bost.

Main Actors: Jean Gabin, Brigitte Bardot, Edwige Feuillère, Nicole Berger,
Franco Interleghi, Madeleine Barbulée, Julien Bertheau.

23) Le baron de l'écluse

France, 1959. (From a short story in a volume entitled *Le bateau d'Emile*, 1954.
It was translated as 'The Idyll Of The Lock' and published once only by Lil-
liput, 1948. The title can be rendered as 'The Baron Of The Lock'.) *Director*:
Jean Delannoy. *Adaptation*: Maurice Druon, Jean Delannoy and Michel
Audiard.

Main Actors: Jean Gabin, Micheline Presle, Blanchette Brunoy, Jean Desailly,
Jacques Castelot, Jean Constantin, Aimé Mortimer.

24) Le président

France, 1961. (*The Premier*, RD78.) *Director*: Henri Verneuil. *Adaptation*:
Henri Verneuil and Michel Audiard.

Main Actors: Jean Gabin, Bernard Blier, Renée Faure, Alfred Adam, Louis
Seigner, Henri Crémieux, Robert Vattier, Charles Cullum.

25) La mort de Belle

France, 1961. (*Belle*, RD64.) *Director*: Edouard Molinaro. *Adaptation*: Jean
Anouilh and Edouard Molinaro.

Main Actors: Jean Desailly, Momique Mélinard, Alexandra Stewart, Jacques
Monod, Yvette Etiévant, Marc Cassot.

Comments: Of particular note in this production is the collaboration with Jean
Anouilh, one of France's most prominent and original playwrights.

26) Le bateau d'Emile

France, 1962. (Based on the untranslated short story 'Le bateau d'Emile', in the
volume entitled *Le bateau d' Emile*, 1954. The title can be rendered as
'Emile's Boat'.) *Director*: Denys de la Patellière. *Adaptation*: Denys de la
Patellière, Albert Valentin and Michel Audiard.

Main Actors: Annie Girardot, Lino Ventura, Pierre Brasseur, Michel Simon,
Jacques Monod, Edith Scob, Joëlle Bernard.

27) L'aîné des Ferchaux

France, 1963. (*The First-Born*, RD46.) *Director*: Jean-Pierre Melville. *Adapta-
tion*: Jean-Pierre Melville.

Main Actors: Jean-Paul Belmondo, Charles Vanel, Michel Mercier, Malvina Sil-
berberg, Stefania Sandrelli, Andrex, Todd Martin.

Comments: A film version of the novel had been planned in 1961 by Jean Valère
and was to star Michel Simon, Alain Delon and Romy Schneider.

28) Trois Chambres à Manhattan

France, 1965. (*Three Beds In Manhattan*, RD48.) *Director*: Marcel Carné. *Adaptation*: Marcel Carné and Jacques Sigurd.

Main Actors: Annie Girardot, Maurice Ronet, Roland Lesaffre, Otto E. Hasse, Gabrielle Fersetti, Geneviève Page, Robert Hoffmann, Margaret Nolan, Virginia Lee.

Comments: For her performance Annie Girardot received the Volpi award for actresses at the Venice Film Festival in 1965. Before giving her the role, Carné had also considered Simone Signoret and Jeanne Moreau. Jean Renoir had considered filming the novel in 1957 with Leslie Caron. Jean-Pierre Melville also planned to film it with Monica Vitti.

29) A Stranger In The House

USA/UK 1967. Also known as *Cop Out*. (*The Strangers In The House*, RD33.) *Director*: Pierre Rouve. *Adaptation*: Pierre Rouve.

Main Actors: James Mason, Geraldine Chaplin, Bobby Darin, Paul Bertoya, Ian Ogilvy, Bryan Stanyon, Pippa Steel, Clive Morton, James Hayter, Meg Jenkins, Marije Lawrence, Moira Lister.

Comments: This was a Dimitri de Grunwald production but distributed by the UK company Rank.

30) Le chat

France, 1971. (*The Cat*, RD95.) *Director*: Pierre Granier-Deferre. *Adaptation*: Pierre Granier-Deferre and Pascal Jardin.

Main Actors: Jean Gabin, Simone Signoret, Annie Cordy, Jacques Rispal, Nicole Desailly, Harry Max, André Rouyer, Carlo Nell, Yves Barsacq.

Comments: A bleak, disturbing film which captures well the atmosphere of the novel. For some inexplicable reason the names of the main characters were changed. Emile and Marguerite have become Julien and Clémence.

31) La Veuve Couderc

France, 1971. (*Ticket Of Leave*, RD39.) *Director*: Pierre Granier-Deferre. *Adaptation*: Pierre Granier-Deferre and Pascal Jardin.

Main Actors: Simone Signoret, Alain Delon, Ottavia Piccolo, Jean Tissier, Monique Chaumette, Bobby Lapointe.

32) Le Train

France, 1973. (*The Train*, RD85.) *Director*: Pierre Granier-Deferre. *Adaptation*: Pierre-Graniere and Pascal Jardin.

Main Actors: Jean-Louis Trintignant, Romy Schneider, Régine, Maurice Biraud, Nike Arrighi, Franco Mazzieri, Serge Marquand.

33) L'horloger de Saint-Paul

France, 1974. (*The Watchmaker Of Everton*, RD70.) *Director*: Bertrand Tavernier. *Adaptation*: Jean Aurenche, Pierre Bost and Bertrand Tavernier.
Main Actors: Pilippe Noiret, Jean Rochefort, Jacques Denis, Julien Bertheau, Sylvain Rougerie, Cécile Vassort, Christine Pascal.
Comments: Obtained the Prix Louis Delluc in 1974. It is a sensitive well-acted film, but purists will find very little of Simenon's sharp dialogue remaining.

34) Der Mörder

Federal Republic of Germany, 1979. (*The Murderer*, RD18.) *Director*: Ottokar Runze. *Adaptation*: Not available.
Main Actors: Gerhard Olschewski, Johanna Liebeneiner, Marius Müller-Westernhagen, Wolfgang Wahl, Uta Hallant.

35) L'Étoile du Nord

France, 1982. (*The Lodger*, RD10.) *Director*: Pierre Granier-Deferre. *Adaptation*: Jean Aurenche, Michel Grisolia and Pierre Granier-Deferre.
Main Actors: Simone Signoret, Philippe Noiret, Fanny Cottençon, Julie Jezequel, Jean Rougerie, Jean-Pierre Klein, Jean-Yves Chatelais.

36) Les fantômes du chapelier

France, 1982. (*The Hatter's Ghosts*, RD56.) *Director*: Claude Chabrol. *Adaptation*: Claude Chabrol.
Main Actors: Michel Serrault, Charles Aznavour, Aurore Clément, Monique Chaumette, Isabelle Sadoyan.
Comments: Apart from noting that the music is by Matthieu Chabrol, it is worth pointing out that a song used in the film was written by Charles Aznavour, who also plays the role of the nervous tailor, Kachoudas.

37) Équateur

France, 1983. (*Tropic Moon*, RD5.) *Director*: Serge Gainsbourg. *Adaptation*: Serge Gainsbourg.
Main Actors: Barbara Sukova, Francis Huster, René Kolldehoff, François Dyrek, Jean Bouise, Julien Guiomar, Roland Blanche, Murray Gronwall.
Comments: Most of the filming was done in the Republic of Gabon, West Africa. The music was also provided by the director.

38) Monsieur Hire

France, 1989. (*Mr Hire's Engagement*, RD4.) *Director*: Patrice Leconte. *Adaptation*: Patrice Leconte and Patrick Dewolf.
Main Actors: Michel Blanc, Sandrine Bonnaire, André Wilms, Luc Thuiller, Erec Bérenger, Marielle Berthon.

39) Betty

France, 1992. (*Betty*, RD84.) *Director/Adaptation*: Claude Chabrol.

Main Actors: Marie Trintignant, Stéphane Audran, Jean-François Garreaud, Yves Lambrecht, Christiane Mainazzoli.

Comments: The film seems to have been quite a family affair: Thomas Chabrol is featured as an actor; the original music was by Matthieu Chabrol; and the script supervisor was Aurore Chabrol.

40) L'inconnu dans la maison

France, 1992. (*The Strangers In The House*, RD33.) *Director*: Georges Lautner. *Adaptation*: Jean Lartéguy, Georges Lautner and Bernard Stora.

Main Actors: Jean-Paul Belmondo, Renée Faure, Ceistiana Réali, Sébastien Tavel, François Perrot, Geneviève Page, Pierre Vernier, Jean-Louis Richard, Gaston Vacchia, Muriel Belmondo.

41) Tsena Golovy

Russia (?), 1992. (Not translated into English. Published originally as *Le prix d'un homme* by Cité, 1980. The title may be rendered as 'A Man's Price'.) *Director/Adaptation*: Nikolai Ilyinsky.

Main Actors: Vladimir Samojlov, Lemnbit Ulfsak, Valentinas Masalskis, Lyubov Poloshchuk, Ivars Kalnins.

42) L'ours en peluche

France, 1994. (*Teddy Bear*, RD83.) *Director*: Jacques Deray. *Adaptation*: Filippo Ascione, Jean Curtelin, Dardano Sacchetti.

Main Actors: Regina Bianchi, Paolo Bonacelli, Martine Brochard, Francesca Dellera, Alain Delon, Julie Du Page, Laure Killing.

Comments: Released as a French film, but with a lot of Italian talent.

43) Tangier Cop

Also known as *Heartbreak City*. USA (?), 1997. (A Simenon novel is credited, but no details are available.) *Director*: Stephen Whittaker. *Adaptation*: Julian Bond.

Main Actors: Donald Sumpter, Pastora Vega, Sean Chapman, Joe Shaw, David Schofield, John Bowler, Claude Aufaure.

44) Los de enfrente

Spain, 1998. (A Simenon novel is credited, and it would seem to be a version of *Les gens d'en face*, which means the same as the Spanish title, and can be rendered as 'The People Opposite' in English. The original English title of the novel was *The Window Over The Way*, RD6.) *Director*: Jesús Garay. *Adaptation*: Jesús Garay.

Main Actors: Carmen Elias, Ben Gazzara, Juanjo Puigcorbé, Estelle Skornik.

45) En plein cœur

Also released in the USA as *In All Innocence*. France, 1998. (*In Case Of Emergency*, RD74.) *Director*: Pierre Jolivet. *Adaptation*: Roselyne Bosch.

Main Actors: Gérard Lanvin, Virginie Ledoyen, Carole Bouquet, Guillaume Canet, Aurélie Vérillon, Jean-Pierre Lorit.

46) Adela

Spain, 2000. (A Simenon novel is credited but no details are available. It would appear to be a version of *Tropic Moon*, RD5, because the main characters in the film, Adèle, or Adela, and Timar, have the same names as those in this novel.) *Director*: Eduardo Mignogna *Adaptation*: Eduardo Mignogna and François-Olivier Rousseau.

Main Actors: Eulalia Ramón, Grégoire Colin, Martin Lamotte, Mario Gas, Isabel Vera, Martín Adjemián.

47) La Habitación Azul

Mexico, 2001. (*The Blue Room*, RD89.) *Director*: Walter Doehner. *Adaptation*: Walter Doehner and Vicente Leñero.

Main Actors: Juan Manuel Bernal, Patricia Llaca, Elena Anaya, Mario Iván Martinez, Margarita Sanz, Damián Alcázar.

6. Simenon On TV And Radio

Maigret On TV

There have been individual TV adaptations of Maigret novels as well as whole series of them in various countries, including France, Italy, Russia, Holland and Japan. However none of these have ever been dubbed or subtitled in English, nor are they likely to be, so information on them is only likely to be of academic interest to an English language audience

It is not generally well known that the first BBC TV Maigret was Basil Sydney in an adaptation of *Maigret And The Young Girl* under the title *Maigret And The Lost Life*. This was broadcast as part of the 'Sunday Night Theatre' series on 4th December, 1959, written by Giles Cooper and produced and directed by Campbell Logan. It lasted 75 minutes and also starred Henry Oscar, Patrick Troughton, Mary Merrall and Andre Van Gyseghem.

The highly successful series of 45/55-minute episodes starring Rupert Davies was to start in October, 1960. Altogether there were 51 episodes by the time the series finished in December, 1963. The very early episodes appear to have been recorded from live studio performances, and the acting is therefore a little insecure at times. Characterisation and atmosphere were however powerfully conveyed. As the series progressed it became technically more accomplished and for Rupert Davies in particular the role came to fit him like a glove. Important features of the series were the exterior sequences filmed on location in Paris; these gave each episode an authentic feel. Six years after the end of the series there was also a special production, in February, 1969, of the novel *Maigret On The Defensive* (under the title *Maigret At Bay*), starring Rupert Davies as Maigret, for the BBC TV *Play Of The Month* series. The later series with Michael Gambon attained this quality of authenticity only occasionally. The locations, many of them in Hungary, always retained something mid-European about them. Michael Gambon however developed a subtle interpretation of the role, combining sensitivity with occasional brusqueness. For most of those who know both the UK Maigret series however, Rupert Davies remains the quintessential Maigret. Simenon once gave Davies a novel inscribed 'At last I have found the perfect Maigret'.

The executive producer for the BBC TV series was Andrew Osborn, though the directors and screenplay writers varied. The regular actors and actresses for the series were as follows: Rupert Davies (Maigret), Ewan Solon (Lucas), Helen Shingler (Madame Maigret), Neville Jason (Lapointe), Victor Lucas (Torrence). Some episodes can be viewed in the BFI archives in London.

The producer for the first Granada TV series (six episodes in 1992) was Jonathan Alwyn, and for the second series (a further six episodes in 1993) it was Paul Marcus. The directors and screenplay writers varied. The regular actors and actresses for both the series were as follows: Michael Gambon (Maigret), Geoffrey Hutchings (Lucas), Jack Galloway (Janvier), James Larking (Lapointe), John Moffat (Coméliau). Ciaran Madden played Madame Maigret in the first six episodes, and Barbara Flynn played her in the second six. All twelve episodes are available in two boxed sets (two tapes in each set): the first series of six, and the second series of six.

The British TV company HTV also produced a one-off two-hour drama entitled *Maigret* in 1988, based on several novels, with Richard Harris as Maigret

BBC Radio Four Maigret Series

The series, the first broadcast in August, 1976 and the last in August, 1977, was set in the framework of Maigret recalling his cases in retirement in an imagined conversation with the author George Simenon. Maurice Denham played Maigret and Michael Gough played Simenon throughout the series.

Despite the presence of two consummate actors playing Maigret and Simenon, the acting rarely comes to life and has the quality of performances in many radio dramas: one can tell the script is being read. There is also much condensation and elimination of many characters and scenes, though the plays remain faithful to the main lines of the plots.

All twelve episodes are available on BBC cassettes in three boxed sets (two cassettes with four episodes in each set).

7. Reference Materials

Simenon Editions

English Language Editions: The main English language editions of Simenon works currently in print are published as 'Harvest Books' by Harcourt Brace & Company, San Diego, New York and London. At the time of this book going to press they are also planning to reissue some editions of Maigret novels with redesigned covers during the centenary year, 2003 (eight in April, and two in each of the months of May, June, July and August). In the Nineties many of the most popular Maigrets and some 'romans durs' were in print as 'Harvest Books'. Penguin UK have the rights to a large number of Maigrets and 'romans durs' which they have published over the years. Recently they have only reissued them to coincide with TV broadcasts of Simenon works (at the time of the Granada *Maigret* series, for example). However twelve Simenons (almost certainly all Maigrets) are scheduled to be reissued by Penguin in 2003 (six in June and six in December). Simenon editions are also occasionally advertised on various online book supply services, such as Amazon.com.

Autobiographies: There have been only three works of autobiography available in English: *When I Was Old* (*Quand j'étais vieux*,1970), published by Harcourt, USA, 1971, Hamilton 1980 and Penguin 3648, 1973; *Letter To My Mother* (*Lettre à ma mere*, 1974), published by Hamilton, 1976, and Harcourt, USA, 1976; and *Intimate Memoirs* (*Mémoires Intimes*, 1981), published by Hamilton, 1984, and Harcourt, USA, 1984.

Biographies

There are many biographical studies available in various languages, but there are only a few in English that readers are likely to find readily available outside specialist libraries. They are listed here in the order of their usefulness to a new reader:

Marnham, Patrick. *The Man Who Wasn't Maigret*, Penguin, 1993. This very stimulating and well-researched book is an enjoyable read.

Assouline, Pierre. *Simenon, A Biography*, Chatto & Windus, 1997. He separates well the fact from the fiction in Simenon's life, but does indulge occasionally in fanciful recreations of scenes himself.

Eskin, Stanley G. *Simenon. A Critical Biography*, McFarland & Co Inc, USA and London, 1987. This contains not only an extensive account of his life but also stimulating reflections on the works.

Bibliography

All of the above books contain useful extensive bibliographies. However, the most useful bibliography in English is that produced by the Dragonby Press:

Foord, Peter. *Georges Simenon, A Bibliography*. No. 3 of 'The Dragonby Bibliographies' by the Dragonby Press, Scunthorpe, England, 1988. This contains a brief biography, alphabetical indexes of separate Maigret and 'romans durs' titles in English and in French, and also lists of the untranslated works. It also includes antiquarian listings of many editions and their market values at the time. This is a must for the serious collector.

Institutions And Societies

Research and archives: Fonds Simenon, Université au Sart-Tilman, Château de Colonster, B-4000 Liège, Belgium, Tel: (41) 56-30-22. Fax: (41) 88-15-55.

For serious students: La Centre d'Ètudes Georges Simenon, Université de Liège, Belgium.

For serious Simenon enthusiasts: Les Amis de Georges Simenon, Secretariat: Michel Schepens, 291, Beigemsesteenweg, 1852-Beigem, Belgium. Tel: (02) 269-47-87. Email: m.schepens@skynet.be

Internet Resources

For Maigret fans there is a dedicated website, with filmographies, book reviews, a bulletin board and other features: www.trussell.com. This site also provides useful links to other sites, most relating to Maigret but some to Simenon in general, in various languages, including French, Italian, German, Finnish, Japanese and Korean, among others. There is also a link to the Fonds Simenon.

The author of this book can be contacted via drcsimenon@hotmail.com

The Essential Library: Currently Available

Film Directors:

Woody Allen (2nd)	**Tim Burton**	**Ang Lee**
Jane Campion*	**John Carpenter**	**Joel & Ethan Coen (2nd)**
Jackie Chan	**Steven Soderbergh**	**Clint Eastwood**
David Cronenberg	**Terry Gilliam***	**Michael Mann**
Alfred Hitchcock (2nd)	**Krzysztof Kieslowski***	**Roman Polanski**
Stanley Kubrick (2nd)	**Sergio Leone**	**Oliver Stone**
David Lynch (2nd)	**Brian De Palma***	**George Lucas**
Sam Peckinpah*	**Ridley Scott (2nd)**	**James Cameron**
Orson Welles (2nd)	**Billy Wilder**	**Roger Corman**
Steven Spielberg	**Mike Hodges**	**Spike Lee**

Film Genres:

Blaxploitation Films	**Bollywood**	**French New Wave**
Horror Films	**Spaghetti Westerns**	**Vietnam War Movies**
Slasher Movies	**Film Noir**	**Hammer Films**
Vampire Films*	**Heroic Bloodshed***	**Carry On Films**
German Expressionist Films		

Film Subjects:

Laurel & Hardy	**Marx Brothers**	**Film Music**
Steve McQueen*	**Marilyn Monroe**	**The Oscars® (2nd)**
Filming On A Microbudget	**Bruce Lee**	**Writing A Screenplay**
Film Studies		

Music:

The Madchester Scene	**Beastie Boys**	**Jethro Tull**
How To Succeed In The Music Business		**The Beatles**

Literature:

Cyberpunk	**Philip K Dick**	**The Beat Generation**
Agatha Christie	**Sherlock Holmes**	**Noir Fiction**
Terry Pratchett	**Hitchhiker's Guide (2nd)**	**Alan Moore**
William Shakespeare	**Creative Writing**	**Tintin**
Georges Simenon		

Ideas:

Conspiracy Theories	**Nietzsche**	**UFOs**
Feminism	**Freud & Psychoanalysis**	**Bisexuality**

History:

Alchemy & Alchemists	**The Crusades**	**The Black Death**
Jack The Ripper	**The Rise Of New Labour**	**Ancient Greece**
American Civil War	**American Indian Wars**	**Witchcraft**
Globalisation	**Who Shot JFK?**	

Miscellaneous:

Stock Market Essentials	**How To Succeed As A Sports Agent**	**Doctor Who**

Available at bookstores or send a cheque (payable to 'Oldcastle Books') to: **Pocket Essentials (Dept GS), P O Box 394, Harpenden, Herts, AL5 1XJ, UK**. £3.99 each (£2.99 if marked with an *). For each book add 50p(UK)/£1 (elsewhere) postage & packing